THE
SOCIAL-EMOTIONAL
GUIDEBOOK:
Motivate Children
With **Social Challenges**
To **Master Social** &
Emotional Coping Skills

THE ART OF
Friendship
SOCIAL-COPING PROGRAM

MICHAEL FOGEL MA, ATR-BC, LPC

author HOUSE®

AuthorHouse™
1663 Liberty Drive
Bloomington, IN 47403
www.authorhouse.com
Phone: 833-262-8899

Published by AuthorHouse 09/14/2020

ISBN: 978-1-7283-5741-6 (sc)
ISBN: 978-1-7283-5740-9 (e)

Library of Congress Control Number: 2020905025

DEDICATION

Dedicated to the memory of my grandparents:

Zayda Sam, Grandma Reba, Grandpa Eugene, and Grandma Sarah,

who loved me just right

CONTENTS

PREFACE

You may think the book you hold in your hands is about social skills training and coaching and the like. Certainly, that's what the cover tells you, but really this book is about love. It is about intentionally delivering acts of love and caring to the world, knowing that the world is a better place when we help each person heal, grow, and reach their vast human potential.

Love is more than an emotion. It's an attitude. And it is not passive; it's more than falling for someone to whom you are attracted. Love can be a philosophy about people and the world. You can *decide* to love. *I decide to love you because you were born and so was I. All I ever needed since I was a baby was to be loved and cared for, and so did you.* Babies need more than the emotion of love. They need acts of caring. Waking up in the middle of the night to hold your child who is throwing up is an act of caring. Driving your friend to the airport or helping them carry an old sofa to the curb is an act of caring. Listening to someone's feelings when they are sad and in the depths of loneliness is an act of caring.

Love is more than an invisible feeling. It can be made visible and manifest in the world through actions that you decide to execute. Cleaning up vomit, carrying a sofa, and listening deeply are all results of an orientation toward love and decisions to act.

But how do we know which acts of love to perform? By understanding exactly what someone needs or wants. Sometimes they explicitly let you know what they need in a personal conversation, a phone call, or a text message. Other times you infer what they need by reading their social cues. "You look sad. Want to talk?" Showing concern for another human being is a way to show a loving orientation to people and the world.

When parenting, teaching, and coaching young people, we must decide to deliver acts I call **Therapeutic Love**. Caring acts with the goal of helping another person heal, learn, and grow, Therapeutic Love, must be given in a manner individualized for each child. We must provide precisely the needed balance of Love (warmth, connection, empathy, teaching, and encouragement) with Limits (boundaries, consequences, and guidance). Unbounded Love is indulgent, like over-watering a houseplant. Love with Limits contributes to healthy relationships and the ideal environment in which a child can learn, grow, and actualize his vast personal potential. You will see the Love with Limits equation come to life throughout this manual.

Deciding to give Therapeutic Love means, "I will learn exactly who you are, I will give you exactly what you need, and I will choose to give you the things you need to heal, grow, and thrive."

I try to live according to this mantra at home as well as with employees, clients, and their parents. Can you imagine if everyone in the world decided one day to give Therapeutic Love to everyone else? This book and the entire Art of Friendship series is my chance to reach even more people with this message. This writing project required incredible investments of time, effort, and energy. It was truly a labor of love. In this book you will find dozens of strategies, scripts, and tips for supporting a young person whom you care about. By choosing to read this book, you are demonstrating your commitment to Therapeutic Love. I hope you extract from it everything you need to help your child.

It just so happens that I had the great fortune to meet a population of young people and families who needed specific kinds of caring acts of love. However, it took me a while to realize it.

When I was in graduate school for art therapy, "Asperger's Syndrome" was not listed in the Diagnostic and Statistical Manual (DSM) of the American Psychological Association. It didn't exist. Without a name, there was no awareness about the needs of this formerly unidentified group of people. In graduate school, I wasn't taught how to help bright, verbal children facing social skills challenges in mainstream settings. When I began working in private practice at the dawn of the twenty-first century, like most people, my experience with developmental disabilities came from the 1988 movie *Rain Man*. In it, Dustin Hoffman's character was an institutionalized adult who may have had more supportive treatment if he had grown up in the present.

As awareness of the new Asperger's Syndrome (AS) diagnosis (and its cousin, Pervasive Developmental Delay, or PDD) burgeoned in the late 1990s and early 2000s, so did the numbers of children and teens frequenting my office who grappled with social engagement and related challenges. They went to mainstream schools but struggled to fit in.

I was dismayed that my clients with AS didn't benefit from the traditional psychotherapy techniques I employed. I hated the feeling of "failing" my clients with PDD and AS. I felt great compassion for their social struggles and identified with them. I remembered from my childhood what it was like to feel different, to have a hard time knowing how to join the group, and to be anxious about speaking to others. As a new father, I also identified with my clients' parents, realizing that the intensity of their love for their child matched my love for my children. I had to help. I had to do a better job of helping. But how? Acts of love.

I endeavored to make a difference. I read everything I could, attended conferences, and integrated best practice social skills training techniques into my art therapy practice. In discovering their needs and striving every day to better meet them, I teased out a method to give my clients exactly what they needed. It turns out that children with other diagnoses also struggle with socialization. I learned that kids with ADHD and learning differences have gaps in their social skills as well.

Children grappling with challenges stemming from all the diagnoses I mentioned benefit from a unique skill-building approach. Years of research and trial and error birthed the approach I lovingly share with you in this book. The crucial ingredients of my program include:

- Direct instruction in social awareness (cognition), emotional awareness (of self and others), and social skills and coping strategies

- Opportunities to practice socialization and emotional coping with a roughly homogeneous, small peer group; social practice occurs in activities ranging from highly structured to less structured, depending on clients' and groups' needs

- Experiences of self-determination through decision making; taking responsibility for successes and mistakes

- Immediate feedback and positive reinforcement to elicit clients' repetition of social-coping skills

- Real-time, compassionate social coaching that illuminates peers' perspectives, connects the child's behavior to peers' reactions, and reinforces the unwritten rules of socialization

- Collaboration with the child's support environment, including parents, educators, and professionals to facilitate generalization of skills

This book, and the rest of the Art of Friendship series, unpacks the many systematized, repeatable acts of caring I developed to meet my clients' social development needs. From these strategies, two programs emerged. The Art of Friendship Social-Coping Program® is a model for outpatient social skills therapy and training. In it, children participate in weekly, hour-long social skills therapy groups after school and on weekends. Its spin-off sibling program, Camp Pegasus, is a therapeutic social skills day camp. Camp Pegasus is an intensive social skills training program embedded in a structured, success-oriented, and fun day camp setting.

My wish is to increase love, compassion, and positivity in our world, which sorely needs it. I happened to develop expertise in working with one unique subset of people, and this is my opportunity to make the world a better place. If you use the techniques with even one child, you will make his life, and therefore the world, better. Teach other parents, caregivers, or professionals what you learn in this volume, and you will make their lives (and their children's) better. Finally, when you are through with this book, don't let it gather dust on your shelf; actively refer to it or pass it on to onto another person who may benefit from it. Share the love.

Together, let's make the world a better place, one child and family at a time.

With Love,

Mike

SECTION 1

CREATING THE FRAME

INTRODUCTION

"I am so worried about my daughter; she has no friends."

"When I try to stop my son's tantrum it gets worse."

"How is my daughter ever going to make it in college if she struggles this way now?."

"Consequences don't work. Nothing seems to work."

"He drives everyone crazy but doesn't realize he's doing it."

"I don't know how to help."

I hope after reading this book, you will have a range of tools to address these concerns and more. My intention is to provide you with unique support skills and strategies so that you feel more competent, more impactful, and more hopeful about your child's social development. This manual outlines many of the techniques that we use in the Art of Friendship Social-Coping Program® and Camp Pegasus. I also recommend many of these ideas in consultations with parents and schools. You will learn a support and training framework that wraps around and cradles your child during the process of social-emotional learning.

Neurodiversity

Dictionary.com defines **neurodiversity** as "the range of differences in individual brain function and behavioral traits, regarded as part of normal variation in the human population (used especially in the context of autistic spectrum disorders)." Neurodiversity was coined by self-advocates, who are adults with Autism. It combats discrimination experienced by high-functioning individuals with Autism engaging in the neuro-typical mainstream world. Neurodiversity offers an accepting and positive connotation for an individual's experience living with social communication differences. Embedded in this wonderful word is the understanding that each person's personality, thoughts, feelings, and behaviors all are differentiated by an almost infinite number of variations of brain wiring. We should accept each person for who he is and how he functions, whether he is functioning neuro-typically, has Autism, uses a wheelchair, is dyslexic, uses a hearing aid, or is blind. We must celebrate each person's gifts and support their efforts to cope with challenges.

The average person, often called **neurotypical,** needs to become aware of, accepting of, and inclusive of the wider range of neurodiverse individuals. We should integrate, collaborate with, and work equitably with the increasingly neurodiverse population that is now integrating into modern society.

In no way am I co-opting the word "neurodiversity," nor do I want to diminish its potency; but I wish we could extend "neurodiversity" to recognize that you and I and all people are neurodiverse. There is great wisdom in that term. It speaks to all of us. (I've grappled with executive functioning skills, I can't remember names at all, and I may have an undiagnosed learning difference in mathematics, myself.) We are all in the same boat, just trying to make it in this world. We all have genetically informed strengths and weaknesses and we should strive to accept each other's different wiring. In my mind, the Golden Rule was never more vital: "Treat others as you would want them to treat you."

Along with all his gifts, the neurodiverse child may have difficulty engaging in age-appropriate activities, be they social, academic, or within the family. Environmental demands may overwhelm the child and cause problems in emotional coping. Social demands may confuse the child and cause problems with interactions with peers or adults. The neuro-diverse person can and will enter mainstream society and, like you and me, strive to function at his personal best. He behaves differently than the average person, and therefore, often faces rejection, discrimination, or marginalization.

Neurodiverse children can experience a great deal of adversity moving out of the nursery and into the neuro-typical social and academic world. Growing up neurodiverse can be hard. Please know that this book is written with love, admiration, and respect for the neurodiverse individual. My campers' and clients' efforts to engage with the mainstream world are inspirational, and they remind me of my own struggles to grow up, fit in, and succeed.

The lessons I teach throughout the Art of Friendship series, and the support strategies I share in this book are never intended to make neurodiverse people feel "less than," defective, or marginalized. Each person has a core, some call it a spirit, that is glorious and special, and I never profess to *change* people. Treatment goals are always to help the child function better, with greater ease, and become the best possible version of *himself*—both for today and for the future. Like you, I pray that your child can emerge from childhood with the best possible self-image, self-efficacy, and confidence.

If you picked up this book, you are the intended audience. Whether you are a parent, grandparent, or other caregiver; whether you are a therapist, support professional, or an educator; you know, love, or work with a neurodiverse child. You are among a group of concerned adults who wish to positively facilitate social-emotional development—and to intervene effectively through rough spots. For clarity and simplicity, this group of adults will be called "caregivers" for the remainder of this book.

As you read this, you may come across a phrase, a strategy, or even a whole section that doesn't resonate. Perhaps certain parts won't fit your child's personality or your family/classroom values. Like I always tell my campers and clients, please don't reject the whole book if one thing or another doesn't fit your needs. This book is a collection of ideas, and I encourage you to read this like a collector. Look for gems scattered throughout that you can use or adapt. Even if you take only one thing from this book, you will be making your child's life better.

Social-Emotional Cognitive Challenges (SECCs)

Michelle Garcia Winner, the well-known grandmother of social skills training, coined the term Social Cognitive Deficits (SCDs) in 2007. SCDs describe social difficulties appearing across diagnoses of that era such as ADHD, Asperger's Syndrome, and Pervasive Developmental Delay. Winner correctly found that these collective conditions are caused by "cognitive deficits". Simply, thay have certain cognitive blind spots, mental distortions, or perceptual errors. Over the years, my group moved away from using the word "Deficits" which connotes something lacking. We reframed them as "social cognitive challenges," SCC's, if you will—a more person-centered term respecting neurodiversity and the struggle—and ability—to overcome. "Social skills groups" is probably the most common term for social skill training in a peer group setting. The wisdom of experience taught me that the terms "SCDs" and "social skills groups" are limiting. They limit our understanding of a child's holistic functioning and they imply that the child is a cognitive-behavior automaton who simply needs to learn and perform social behaviors.

What about the soul of the child? What about his lived emotional and sensory experience? Over time, my group added to the SCC concept the word "emotional," because social skills do not occur in isolation. Over thousands of hours facilitating social skills therapy with children, I noticed simultaneous emotional overreactions, distortions, and eruptions. Inner tensions or emotions contribute to children's dysregulated feelings and behaviors. Strong feelings spark instinctive impulses to act. Biological instincts (fight, flight, and freeze for example) don't play well in social groups or relationships. I always say, "You can't do social if you're freaking out." In light of this discovery, I coined the descriptor, **Social-Emotional Cognitive Challenges (SECCs)**. Our services offer "**Social-Coping Skills**" featuring direct instruction and practice in both social skills *and* emotional coping skills.

SECCs are clusters of social-emotional traits that concentrate on the following areas: cognitive processing (learning and understanding), executive functioning (organizing, sequencing, inhibiting impulses), social communication/social cognition (reading social cues, inferring others' perspective, pragmatic language), emotion awareness/management, and sensory integration. Because of my therapy and counseling training, my dual focus includes biological (wiring) factors as well as emotional (psychological, coping) factors.

Many kids who need help with social skills and emotional coping skills do not have a formal psychiatric diagnosis. A person qualifies for a psychiatric diagnosis when coping skills gaps cluster strongly around one (or more) functional area and then get in the way of his functioning. The child may receive a diagnosis such as ADHD, High Functioning Autism, learning differences, or other, less common neuro-developmental (brain-based) disorders.

When I talk about the child with SECCs, I refer to "the child" or "your child." When talking about children and teens I use the terms "child," "youth," "children," "student," and "kid" interchangeably. Also, regarding my use of pronouns, when I provide examples of behavior or skills, "he" and "his" alternate with "she" and "hers" from chapter to chapter.

The support strategies contained in this book were originally designed to meet the needs of children with SECCs. However, parents and teachers tell us that neurotypical children and children with emotional support needs quickly benefit from Social-Coping Skill instruction and coaching, as well. The difference is neurotypical children tend to simply need the tips, but with less intensity and repetition to acquire social and coping skills.

The children who will most benefit from this book experience neurologically based SECCs. They misread social cues, feel anxious or angry, and wind up isolated, ostracized, teased, or bullied. Their social challenges (and special gifts) stem from a unique mental processing style - like a social learning difference—that requires a specific treatment approach. The children we serve are often excellent at learning and retaining visual and active social skills lessons. The devil is in the execution of these new social skills in the real world.

What impedes execution of behavior in general and social skills specifically? Impulsiveness and weaker self-regulation short-circuit the best-laid plans. Impulsiveness makes it impossible to stick to a plan. Plans often consist of a sequence of steps: "First I will do X, then I will do Y, then I will do Z." Impulsive children may exuberantly forget to do X, and the rest of the plan dissolves. If an interesting distraction pops into the impulsive child's mind, the child may do Q, or maybe he skips X, and then performs step Y five times in a row, louder and louder. Impulsiveness happens to be exacerbated by emotion, even positive emotion. The child with self-regulation challenges may become elated and silly when happy, and his fight-flight-freeze response may get activated by everyday experiences.

Indeed, weakness in social skills often comes with other challenges, such as regulating emotions, impulses, and behaviors. Feelings such as anxiety or frustration overflow, causing children to act out their distress behaviorally. In my experience, it is not enough to teach a child a social skill only, because emotions and impulses may block his ability to execute it. If it were so simple, we would just ask the child with SECCs to "Improve this behavior" or "Stop doing that behavior." Many children simply *can't* change their behavior on demand. Some children do not (yet) have the self-awareness or self-control in real time to change based solely on a helpful tip. Not only do feelings get in the way of successful socialization, but emotional and sensory flooding triggers instinctive behaviors that may clash with social or classroom expectations.

If your child could socialize or behave "better," *he would*. The lay public will often misunderstand a child with SECCs. People just don't realize that he can't help it. Most adults who don't spend a lot of time with children with SECCs erroneously ascribe intent and meaning to the child's behavior. "That kid's mean." "He is doing that on purpose." "His parents have no control over him." "What a jerk." "He doesn't care about anyone but himself." That's a lot of negative judgement that can weigh on anyone.

I'm sure you experience society's pressure to have your child behave in a conventional way—like "most kids should." You witness inappropriate behavior or get an email from your child's teacher and respond the way you were taught since you were a child—with old-school discipline, lectures, or consequences. The parenting and classroom management techniques that work with neurotypical children often don't work with the child with SECCs.

If you feel societal pressure for your child to blend in, cooperate, and connect, you may cultivate a subconscious (or conscious) sense of desperation. In your urgency to stem the behavior quickly, *your* mind may adopt value judgments. You might lapse into black-and-white thinking, which breaks things down into polarities of good and bad, or in-control versus out-of-control. I call this binary-behavioral thinking, which is a dead end for your child and your relationship with your child.

You want to address "bad," disruptive or out-of-control behavior ASAP—preferably yesterday. You ratchet up the consequences or your volume, but your increasingly intense interventions cause pain and frustration, conflict and tension, rejection and distance. Worst of all, they don't work. Your child probably does not stop the behavior in question, and he doesn't learn new ways to behave. The old way isn't netting the results you desire. A part of you may feel hopeless and you may want to throw your hands in the air and give up. You know that isn't the answer, but what is a caregiver to do?

Your child's mixed neurological and emotional differences demand a specific and unique approach. The support strategy you develop needs to take into consideration all the child's abilities and cognitive differences. We need to build on his uncommon strengths and compensate for blind spots in his mental processing profile. To move forward, your child needs all the adults in his life to adopt a developmental focus with a teaching and coaching mindset.

Your child needs to learn positive replacement social-coping skills to handle life's frustrations. Then, he needs a village of supportive caregivers to reinforce and support the acquisition of those skills. Most social skills practitioners assert, and the research agrees, that the best social-coping skills training must occur across the therapist-home-school settings.

This book provides you and your child's support network the skills to do just that. Imagine feeling competent and confident in helping your child grow toward your dreams for him—and his goals for himself. We want your child to dream dreams for himself, and to make them come true.

That is my wish for you and for your child. I hope that you will find at least one—if not five or ten—actionable strategies that will empower you and make your child's life better.

The book is broken into two sections. Section 1 introduces the subject of social-coping skills training and promotes an ultra-positive and compassionate approach emanating from the Person-Centered/Humanistic tradition of therapy. Many children with social skills challenges find themselves in **negative feedback cycles** with the world. This section proposes the imperative for and the means to reverse that negative cycle and make it positive. Section 1 encompasses chapters one and two. Chapter 1 focuses on social-coping skills development in a holistic and humanistic framework. Chapter 2 covers understanding levels of frustration/brain arousal and supporting emotions in service of social-coping skills training.

Section 2 gets into the nuts and bolts of social-coping skills training. It teaches practical strategies to reinforce pro-social behaviors, discourage negative ones, and coach children through social miscues. Chapter 3 describes ways to deliver Therapeutic Love in the form of an ultra-positive reinforcement and behavior support program. Chapter 4 details strategies and scripts to guide caregivers' social-emotional coaching and problem-solving efforts. Chapter 5 illuminates misconceptions of, and realistic implementation of limits and boundaries. It differentiates unacceptable behaviors from social mistakes.

Enjoy.

CHAPTER 1

CHILD-CENTERED SOCIAL-COPING SKILL DEVELOPMENT

Many children with SECCs have a village of helpers working to support their social and emotional growth. Unfortunately, when multiple helpers are involved, they might not all communicate and coordinate their efforts with one another. Multiple approaches and voices can confuse the child with SECCs. Successful social and coping skill development requires that, when possible, you build a unified approach among your child's support team. We can honor each person's personality, effort, training, and opinion and still develop a team with one set of support guidelines. I hope you will spread the ideas in this book to the various support team members and caregivers in your child's life.

Many of my clients face challenges navigating their daily schedule. Wake up, organize yourself to get dressed and out the door on time. Take the wild and loud bus ride to school. Once you arrive, you face six hours of subject and room transitions; demands on attention and performance; peers expecting you to converse, play and compromise; requirements to sit still; a barrage of sight, sound, kinesthetic, tactile, and smell sensory input; and the even wilder bus ride home.

Your child tries her hardest to fit in and function, and the effort to hold it all together is exhausting. On top of that, she faces heightened emotions due to her SECCs. There is the anxiety of raising her hand to participate or ask for help, the worry that she may not get a seat in the cafeteria next to her most comfortable peer, the sadness when she gets to the recess yard late (due to a slow transition) and there are no more positions for her in the game. The student sitting next to your child swings her foot all the time and it drives your child crazy, and then it is time for your child's most hated subject: forty-five minutes of hell trying to come up with an idea for one paragraph to free-write.

On top of that, your child may be receiving subtle negative messages from teachers or peers. "Emily, please go back to your seat. Back to your seat. Emily, head back to your seat. Emily you are out of your seat. Emily, what are you doing in the cubby area? Please return to your seat. Emily ... Emily... Emily." Redirection all day, even with the best of intentions, communicates to the child, "You are off task. You are wrong … wrong … wrong." Caregivers' voices certainly become impatient the seventh time they redirect the child. This feels like a negative cycle. Emily may feel as though she can't do anything right and that you don't like her.

There may be negative cycles with peers, as well. Some peers may nonverbally communicate rejection by turning their backs on Emily. Other rejection may be more overt, "Emily you can't join our recess club." "Go away. You're so annoying." During group projects, "Darn. Do I have to be paired with Emily?"

Now Emily goes home and is mentally drained, only to have to cope with "annoying siblings" (her words), chores, homework, and dinnertime. Many kids in my program hold it together at school and then take it out on family after school. Countless caregivers report after school crying, tantrums, meanness to siblings, defiance, homework battles or arguments over bedtime. Guess what that elicits in caregivers? More redirection and correction. Your child thinks, "I can't catch a break." Several children have been able to put into words, "What's the point of living … it's all so hard. I stink at everything."

Repeated frustration and experiences perceived as failure erode a child's confidence. If we don't interrupt the negative cycle, children will adopt negative attitudes toward themselves. "I can't" and "Why even try?" are emblematic statements of learned helplessness. Other negative statements such as, "No one likes me," "I'll never do well in school," and "I'll never make a friend" are seeds for the development of emotional disorders like anxiety and depression.

Emily desperately needs compassion. Yes, she needs to build a lot of social-emotional skills to function better. Reactive correction only grinds her spirit down. Many parents invoke one version or another of this sentiment: "My child is going to be an amazing adult with all her gifts. We just have to get her there." That is true, though I must add, "Not only do we have to get her there, but with her self-concept and self-esteem intact, so that she can enjoy all that adult life and relationships have to offer."

Together, we can do something about the negative feedback loop your child experiences. It's not too late. What can we do? It starts with Therapeutic Love: compassion and understanding. It involves the creation of a unified collaboration between home and school caregivers. The negative cycle turns positive with the right environmental accommodations, and by establishing meaningful interventions that give Emily the tools to succeed.

Holistic View

Social-coping skill development is sometimes mistakenly thought of as teaching a discrete set of concrete skills, such as folding laundry. Folding a shirt in your bedroom has repeatable steps as easy as one, two, three. But what if it were more complicated than that? Learning social skills is not as easy as folding a shirt, one, two, three.

Imagine you were folding a shirt on a raft in roiling waves with whipping wind during a thunderstorm. There is a lot more to it than folding, one, two, three. You try to keep your balance and worry that you might fall. You need to account for the wind having unpredictably undone your last fold; it's so frustrating. That thunder is so loud; it drives you to distraction. You fear the unknown. "Will lightning strike?" "Will I make it home?" That is closer to the experience of a child with SECCs who tries to practice newly learned social-coping skills. There's a lot going on around and inside your child while she tries to execute.

The caring adult declares, "I'm teaching my kid social skills." We teach social cognition, perspective-taking, hidden social rules, and tips for engagement. Those skills are the foundation of social skill development. However, using *only* a highly cognitive social skills curriculum without addressing the trainee's emotional experience – and regulation- is overly mechanical and dehumanizing. In my experience, it is a recipe for unsuccessful training. People are three-dimensional beings, and we must consider the whole person. While my program is known for teaching social skills concretely and effectively, we never overlook the whole child.

It's not enough to teach social skills without teaching emotional coping skills. If your child is freaking out or tantrum-ing, she can't practice socializing better.

Nor is it enough to teach **social skills** and **emotional coping skills** without concentrating on other neurodevelopmental areas, such as developing pragmatic language (negotiation and assertiveness), managing sensory experiences (sensory integration), and strengthening executive function skills (sequencing, cause-and-effect, and problem solving).

Finally, we're missing something if we exclusively address social, emotional, and neurodevelopmental issues if we don't also focus on your child's behavior. We want to decrease the negative feedback loop from the world, but not to the extent that we make apologies and excuses for unacceptable behaviors. We need to hold kids accountable for their behavior, right? The problem is, with exclusively behavioral approaches the child's emotional experience is minimized. A hyper-focus on changing behavior makes the child feel like she's a 'science project', crushing her spirit.

In this book, I discuss **shaping behavior**. Behaviorism goes back to B.F. Skinner and his theories that human behavior is dictated by positive or negative outcomes. In other words, we do things for expected rewards or avoid doing things to avoid negative consequences. Parts of this book borrow concepts from behaviorism. For example, you will read about the imperative to provide verbal positive reinforcement. I include an option to add a behavior modification system using a token-based reward system to motivate and reinforce the practice of social-coping skills. You will even learn how to leverage specific consequences to decrease the repetition of unacceptable behavior.

However, over-focusing on behavior is also reductionist and loses sight of the complete child, with emotions, sensory experiences, and cognitive strengths and gaps. Behaviorism is only one small tool in a holistic toolbox of strategies for social-coping skill training. It does not account for the "soul" and the intent of your child's good heart. Behaviorism doesn't adequately account for actions a child performs during a meltdown. Alone, it doesn't provide for the gaps in social-emotional cognitive skills. Behavior, therefore, is another part of the solution, but not the be-all and end-all.

Thus far, I discussed behavior as activated by internal tensions and emotions. Let's not stop there. What about the other partner in the feedback loop—the environment? Our ideal social-coping skills training model must not ignore powerful influences on the child's life and growth like parents, caregivers, peers, and school. Powerful social-coping skills trainers view caregivers and educators as resources. We must reach out to one another and build support skills among the whole team. Let's holistically wrap our collective arms around your whole child's whole world—with compassion and positivity.

The Art of Friendship Embraces the Philosophy of "AND"

We focus on Social Skills,

AND we focus on Emotional-Coping Skills,

AND we focus on sensory issues, executive functioning needs, and language development,

AND we focus on your child's self-concept and perception of others,

AND we focus on behavior,

AND we focus on your child's spirit, strengths, and gifts,

AND we focus on caregivers such as parents, educators, and professionals.

This is why I named my therapy practice the Art of Friendship Social-Coping Skills Program®. Our program fuses social cognition and skills with the emotional-coping skills required to engage with life. Join me in establishing a holistic culture of "AND." This book is about how you provide holistic, compassionate Social-Coping Skills training and support.

Effective social-coping skills training involves the creation of a safe, predictable environment in which children receive:

- Direct instruction in social awareness, strategies, and skills

- Direct instruction in emotional-coping awareness, strategies, and skills

- Instruction and practice of assertiveness and pragmatic communication skills

- Instruction, modeling, and experience in effective problem-solving skills

- Opportunities to practice social skills with peers

- Behavioral reinforcement of effective social skills (as needed)

- Compassionate coaching approach for social/behavioral mistakes

- Nonjudgmental opportunities to calm down and re-regulate before coaching or demands are reactivated.

Child-Centered Adults

One of my heroes, Carl Rogers, founded **Person-Centered (Humanistic) Therapy** in the mid-twentieth century. Person-centered philosophy is widespread and universal in education, medicine, multiculturalism, and in nearly every approach to psychotherapy.

Being humanistic, or person-centered, means:

- Trusting that all people have an innate drive to heal, grow, and develop toward their individual potential.

- Believing that all people have self-determination—the capacity to make choices to direct their lives in positive directions.

- Unconditional positive regard, which is acceptance that we are all doing our best to function on any given day. Some days are better than others, some circumstances are worse than others. Sometimes the world creates obstacles, but we are *all* trying to make our way each day. Regardless of *how* someone is doing, we accept *who* she is.

- Accepting that sometimes the world calls on us to do things for which we don't yet have the skills to achieve social, academic, or business success. In this case there is nothing "wrong" with you or me or my young clients. The child can return to her developmental path by learning the critical skills for success.

Person-centered caregivers, teachers, and therapists can help the child return to her developmental path in four key ways:

- Helping the child identify, accept, and trust her emotions, and recognize that they are helpful guides

- Pointing out and reinforcing the child's innate capacity to powerfully direct her life

- Initially removing environmental obstacles and stressors that are too big for the child to overcome (initial success-oriented accommodation) and reintroducing them when the child is ready

- Teaching positive, replacement social-coping skills that empower and enable the child to achieve social and academic success

Person-Centered Therapy led naturally to **Child-Centered Therapy**. If you are child centered, you begin by differentiating that children are not miniature adults. Childhood has its own experiences, mental/physical capabilities, and roles. If Person-Centered Therapy strives to accept the individual where she is, then Child-Centered Theory strives to understand exactly what childhood entails and demands and what each individual child needs.

Child-Centered Therapy similarly always believes that children—all children—strive to function their best. When children chronically struggle emotionally or behaviorally, it reveals that something is blocking their natural developmental path.

Presently, with decades of brain research and understanding of neurodevelopmental disorders, we have an idea of what blocks the path of the child with neurodevelopmental disorders. The obstacle is formed by the Social-Emotional Cognitive Challenges (SECCs).

Children develop abilities and skills in a sequential, developmental manner. Cognitive (processing) challenges disrupt the organic and sequential developmental sequence. Gaps form in social, problem-solving, communication, and emotional-coping skills. Sadly, these cognitive-skill gaps are revealed behaviorally when a child struggles to initiate and sustain play or conversation, argues with peers, explodes in rage, or avoids enriching experiences out of anxiety. It's not the child's fault. The fact that it's not the child's fault cannot be emphasized enough when brain-based processing differences create skill gaps.

It is these very gaps that can injure confidence and diminish resilience and self-esteem over time. Repeated frustration or failure experiences created by social-coping skills gaps create destructive negative feedback cycles between the child and her world. It's not her fault.

I'm sure you always try your best to maintain basic self-regulation, feel good, and meet environmental expectations. I do, too. But sometimes we function better, and other times, worse, depending on factors such as tiredness, hunger, environmental demands, and stress. If you are asked to do something and you don't know how to do it, you don't want to be judged or yelled at; you want someone to show you how. Stop for a moment, take that in, and reflect. Your child feels the same way.

This piece of empathy generates deep compassion for the child's struggle and is a crucial feature of the Art of Friendship orientation to childhood. It can be hard to grow up. *We must accept who the child is today, with a hopeful eye for growth and improvement tomorrow.*

Person-centered theory has become so ubiquitous that it has entered popular culture. Many people assume that they know about it. Perhaps they think it is a pie-in-the-sky "up with people" theory. "Am I supposed to assume that everyone is good? That's not true." Correction: the person-centered practitioner does not accept bad behavior. I work with the client and explore the client's evaluation of the behavior. I trust that the client will eventually discover the core issue, and then rework and repair the obstacle from the inside. This leads to the client developing self-awareness, and the capacity for self-determination to choose not to do the inappropriate behavior again. Everyone can participate in this process.

When an idea reaches popular culture, nuance and detail are sometimes washed away and only its most superficial notions are remembered. "Okay, so I show unconditional positive regard and meet her where she is, and she'll suddenly get better? This person-centered stuff is nice and encouraging and all, but … so what?" If you didn't study this approach, you might not know that to practice person-centered engagement, there are simple and clear ways of communicating and listening. Rogers believed that therapists' **empathy** was the most important factor in therapy. He defined empathy in action, as true, deep, non-judgmental **listening**.

Empathic listening as an act of Therapeutic Love is externalized by verbally and nonverbally reflecting what the client says and does. **Reflection** is more than a mechanical technique to use *on* someone. It is an act of *caring*. It is an attitude about relationships and a way of being *with* someone. Being person-centered this way is like holding up a mirror to your counterpart. In Child-Centered Therapy, you become the mirror. Your consistent observation, along with brief statements to the child of what you see makes you the mirror. You become the reflective object that empowers, trains, and liberates your child. Become the mirror. Give it a try. When you try any new skill, at first you feel weird, then a little wobbly, until finally, you produce mirroring statements easily and steadily. I'll break it down for you.

Benefits of Reflection

A reflective approach brings wonderful benefits. It communicates deep acceptance of who the child is. It provides positive attention to children who often feel criticized and rejected. Mirroring the child disarms her need to engage in power struggles because you demand less and observe more. Heavy reflection helps the child see herself—her feelings, her behaviors. All of that leads to self-awareness and self-determination. You activate multiple levels of emotional and behavioral learning when you reflect your child's behavior.

Emotional learning

Self-awareness: Reflecting and labeling your child's emotional states (versus behaviors, which will be discussed shortly) helps her identify common triggers for specific emotions, the vocabulary to describe her concerns, and body tensions/sensations. The child lacking emotion awareness doesn't know why she gets upset and can't predict when her next implosion or explosion will happen. She is reactive and may roller-coaster through life from one meltdown to the next. Deficits in self-awareness create difficulty with empathy and concern for others' needs. The un-aware child may bother or insult others and set herself up for rejection. Additionally, the child without emotion awareness is frequently shocked, unprepared, and confused when she experiences *any* feeling, causing her to react impulsively. The development of self-awareness allows for the release of feelings, consideration of others, and self-control. Saying things like, "You sound really frustrated." or "You look sad. What do you need?" helps the child realize what she is feeling. Emotions are our guides. They constitute the first step in you and your child understanding what her experience is and what she wants and needs. See the feeling and say the feeling.

Affective communication (emotional vocabulary): Babies through preschoolers learn to label and categorize their emotions, impulses, and behaviors through feedback from others, especially adult caregivers. When a baby cries two hours after eating, the attuned caregiver says, "You must be hungry." With repetition, the child attaches the label "hungry" to the inner sensation of hunger. Eventually, the child links the feeling of hunger to assertive language, saying, "I'm hungry." Suddenly the caregiver is able to meet the child's needs. We tend to stop labeling kids' experience after the preschool years, because we think that type of talk sounds babyish.

Developing an affective vocabulary not only helps with communication of emotional state and needs, but it also creates mental "cubbies" in which to organize, understand, and remember her experiences. When your child hears you reflect her emotional state, a) she becomes aware of it, and b) she can mentally associate it with similarly labeled experiences. "Oh, I remember that I felt sad two other times around Gracie. I realize that Gracie makes me feel sad a lot. The sense of mental organization and mastery decreases your child's sense of emotional confusion and overwhelm. "Maybe I won't play with Gracie anymore." This breeds self-regulation and self-assurance.

Acceptance and trust in emotions: Many people fear their emotions and are imprisoned by them. Why? Because the young person who frequently melts down *learns* that she is constantly emotionally flooded. She hates losing control like that and judges her meltdowns as "bad." Feelings are perceived as the "evil villains" that spoil your child's good mood. Instinctively, your child grows vigilant and fearful of experiencing uncomfortable feelings.

She develops the psychological instinct to "stuff" them inside and never talk about them, causing two maladaptive outcomes. First, the obvious one: stuffed feelings always seek release. Trapped feelings build and, with little provocation, explode like a volcano. Children who defend against feelings seem emotionally brittle and unpredictable. Peers and adults tiptoe around them so as not to cause an eruption.

The second consequence of disconnecting from feelings is less dramatic but no less dangerous. Your child becomes highly avoidant of emotional discomfort, which is a necessary ingredient for growth and maturation. She refuses to deal with important challenges and avoids making mistakes for fear of being overwhelmed. She has low resilience that discourages her from taking the safe social risks required to advance her towards maturity and independence.

Child-centered reflection can help your child overcome the fear of emotion and avoidance. Your reflection of the child's full range of feelings and behaviors neutralizes their threat. "I've been nervous most times I tried something new. I survived it each time. I'll probably be okay if I try this new activity." Reflection is normalizing and debunks the idea that all feelings are bad and must be stuffed. I call it "making friends with feelings."

Preparation for assertiveness: After children develop emotional awareness and affective language—and after they "make friends with feelings"—they are positioned for the development of assertiveness skills. Assertiveness skills bring huge benefits. "I want ... " or "I need ... " statements reduce or prevent meltdowns, decrease anxiety and avoidance, increase social and academic success, and multiply confidence and self-esteem. These are made possible by your adoption of child-centered reflection of the child's needs and wants. "Oh, you want_____." or "Now I understand, you need _____." helps your child identify her underlying need and want, and you can coach her to use language to get it met. Assertiveness scripts (our "Power of I" assertiveness lesson) can be taught to initiate assertiveness. Have your child say, "I feel_____, I need _____, I'd like you to _____."

Preparation for problem solving: First, you labeled internal states. Your child is now able to say, "I'm angry about this." "This assignment is confusing." "I feel lonely and excluded by my friends." The next step in reflection connects the child's experience of frustration with the need for relief from frustration. Notice how your reflection turns to problem solving with the addition of one additional sentence in the form of a question. Say, "You look frustrated. How do you want to handle this?" Or, "You seem overwhelmed by this assignment. Do you want some help getting started?" Or, "You look stuck, let's solve this problem. What are three things you might try to handle this?" Start with reflection, development of an affective vocabulary and identification of emotional states in the body. Then, add on problem-solving and your child's quality of life just exploded in a positive way.

Discovery of self-determination and choice: Every behavior and non-behavior is a choice—whether it is conscious or unconscious. Young children and unaware/impulsive older children don't realize this fact. When you make reflecting comments on the behavioral level (as opposed to emotions, previously discussed), you emphasize and validate the choice your child just made. "You decided to _____." "You chose to _____." Your positive comments of these decision moments help your child become aware of all the large and small decisions your child makes throughout the day. Frame and reinforce them with your reflective words so your child learns that she has self-determination. Your enthusiastic reflection of choice communicates, "That was great. Now, can you harness that decision and do it again?"

Subtle shaping of desired traits and behaviors: As we teach our clients and campers, nonverbal communication conveys most of your intended meaning. Your words and tone of voice in reflecting your child's behavior and decisions defines its meaning. You can strategically reframe your child's behavior in terms of positive characteristics, traits, or behaviors you want her to repeat. For instance, your child may interpret a homework session in terms of how frustrating and stressful it was. She may not be aware that there is another way to think about the ninety minutes of hard work she just completed. You might reflect it by emphasizing her great determination and persistence. Reflect and describe what you see: "You are showing such perseverance; keep going." or "You didn't give up. You powered through that hard math worksheet." Look how your reflective words reframe and define the experience in terms of developing positive skills/traits. Reframed reflection directs your child's attention to the efficacious behaviors and traits you would love her to develop and repeat. You are catching and validating the real positives of which your child is capable. With that awareness, your child can harness that capability and try to use it intentionally.

Development of cause-and-effect thinking and productive evaluation of behavioral and social choices: In addition to reflecting your child's behavioral choices, you should also reflect the outcomes of behavior. You needn't make the evaluation for your child—save that for her. Reflective comments of outcomes include statements such as, "Did you notice that when you gave Sean that heartfelt apology, he stopped calling you names?" or, "Remember when you didn't talk to your friend for three weeks after she hurt your feelings? Now it seems as though she doesn't feel like inviting you to her birthday party." Reflect the outcomes you see but your child can't. Your reflection of social cause-and-effect over time helps your child understand that she can invite positive or negative outcomes based on the behavior she chooses.

After you verbally reflect your child's action and how it turned out, ask her to evaluate it. "Did you like that or not?" or "How's that working out for you?" If it worked out well, congratulate your child. "That worked out great for you. Do that again the next time something like this happens." Build on the successes.

On the other hand, if your child does not like the outcome, brainstorm together with her. What could make things better? "Remember when you didn't talk to your friend for three weeks after she hurt your feelings? It seems as though she didn't feel like inviting you to her birthday party. It looks like you are the only one who got hurt after you ignored her. If you want her to think you are still interested in being her friend, you might want to do something different. What could you start doing tomorrow at school?" We all build on successes and learn from our mistakes. Your child with SECCs requires help productively evaluating her choices. Notice how reflective comments make outcome evaluation possible.

Grow your child's independence: Reflective comments to the child are all about "you …You … YOU" (where *you* is the child). Place the responsibility for thinking socially and making good choices squarely in your child's hands. When you provide instructions, evaluations, or solve problems for your child, who does the thinking? You do. Your child knows it and feels it. It decreases her sense of autonomy and self-efficacy. Why should your child think when you do the heavy lifting? Instead reflect, reflect, reflect, and ask, ask, ask your child how she wants to proceed. Give her the gift and responsibility of social-coping thinking. "You look bored. What do you want to do?"

Less frequent power struggles: You will notice that with your child-centered engagement, the child has fewer things to oppose. Think about it this way: when you direct or command, you are a firm object against which your child can push back. She can debate, argue, or refuse your position. Those times that defiance does flare up, reflection completely disarms it. "Wow. You really don't want to get ready for bed. I hear you loud and clear, but look what time it is."

You lead with empathy and your child will feel your compassionate understanding, even while you hold firm on the direction to go to bed. She will interpret your coaching as supportive and gain a sense of personal awareness, responsibility, and power. "You are locked up and stuck. I'm sure you will get unstuck soon." Notice the tone. Notice how you come off as congruent and neither adversarial nor commanding.

Feedback from educators, parents, and even young clients tells us that kids become more manageable, less combative, and more open to learning social-coping skills when they feel truly understood. In my program, we find that holding up a mirror to the child's feelings and behavior creates the ideal environment for learning, empowerment, and growth.

Reflection ties into the Art of Friendship Social-Coping behavior reinforcement system: As you read further into this book, you will learn about a positive behavior reward system to invigorate social-coping skills practice in your child. Child-centered reflection and facilitative questioning lie at the heart of our ultra-positive training and coaching approach.

An inevitable question always follows when I present this material: "This seems abstract. You gave some pointers, but how do I *act* child centered?" The next section details how you can achieve the child-centered engagement and relationship I described. You will learn how to achieve the ultra-compassionate supportive tone we preach and practice. The following methods of reflective observation and communication may be employed in a wide range of situations and settings. After you read each section, try to imagine actual past (and future) interactions in which you might use each type of reflective comment with your child.

To begin, I will introduce you to two levels of reflective comments. Level one reflection can be thought of as superficial, or surface comments about what you observe. Level two reflection is "deeper" because it focuses on your child's internal experience, including feelings, thoughts and needs.

Level 1 Reflection consists of **tracking comments** you can use most of the day, every day. This is the default setting, which is applicable most of the time. Simply, you say what you see, hear, and know. Your observations reflect your child's behavior, choices, outcomes, and skills. Tracking comments observe behaviors from the visible tip of the iceberg, above the surface. Tracking comments are great for developing awareness of self-determination in your child because you announce all the choices your child makes throughout the day.

Deeper, Level 2 Reflection is made up of **mirroring comments.** Mirroring comments reflect emotions, activity/energy level, thoughts, wants, needs, and motivations both in your child and others with whom she interacts. Mirroring comments help the child develop emotion awareness and an affective vocabulary. They make emotions less threatening to experience and discuss. Mirroring comments of emotion also illuminate triggers to impulses and motivation that lie beneath the surface. Here is how to use tracking comments and mirroring comments:

Level 1 tracking comments reflect the child's decisions, behavior, and outcomes. Like holding up a word mirror, keep saying what you concretely see and hear the child doing.

Sample tracking comments about your child's behavior:

- "You are not giving up."

- "You held the door for everyone ... that was so kind."

- "You were so flexible just now."

- "You are not ready to turn off the TV."

- "You are taking a break from your homework."

Tracking comments to raise your child's awareness of others' behavior:

- "Jimmy decided to let you go first."

- "Emily held her hand out to create space because you were too close."

- "You had a turn before, and now Sam is taking his turn."

- "Most of the kids in your class are playing soccer during recess."

- "Your teammates are huddling up to listen to the coach's instructions."

Tracking comments to raise your child's awareness of her capacity for self-determination:

- "You decided to let your friend go first."

- "You chose to take a break from your homework and get right back to it when you are calm."

- "You changed your mind and said yes to your friend's invitation."

- "You refused to give up on learning to ride your bike and now you can do it."

- "You did not let that morning argument ruin your day."

Tracking comments to raise your child's awareness of social cause-and-effect:

- "You decided to let Jimmy go first; look how happy it made him. Because you did that for him, now he wants to let you pick the next game."

- "You kept talking about Yu-Gi-Oh cards the whole time. Did you notice that your friend's eyes started wandering around the room for a minute and then he left your conversation? He got tired of listening to the same topic for so long."

- "You decided to punch your sister and that means you decided to have a time out on this chair for five minutes. Hurting behaviors automatically lead to a time out."

- [To tweens and teens] "You snuck your phone into your room which is against our family's rules. You lose your phone whenever you break our family's terms of use."

- You posted that offensive meme to social media and now the other kids are un-following you."

Level 2 mirroring comments reflect the child's mood, emotion, and arousal (level of frustration/ anger). You can provide deeply felt empathy by listening for and reflecting obvious emotional states, both verbal and non-verbal. Children feel deeply understood when you mirror the feelings evoked by their words, body language, and tone of voice. Empathic mirroring gets to the root of affect like frustration, anger, jealousy, and other feelings that make kids act out negatively. Sometimes a well-placed mirroring comment can neutralize a strong feeling and allow the child to regulate herself, which makes problem-solving possible. Here are examples of mirroring comments:

Mirroring comments to develop emotion awareness:

- "That sounds sad."

- "Your feelings got hurt when she said that."

- "You are furious."

- "You are worried about _____."

- "You can really use a hug right now."

Mirroring comments to raise awareness of others' emotional states:

- "Jimmy sounds really annoyed right now. Listen to his voice."

- "Emily's feelings got hurt when you said, 'Your glasses look weird.' Look at her face."

- "Sam is running around wildly. He is pretty hyper and his engine is running fast."

- "Look around, most of the kids at lunch are staying at the table, eating, chatting, and listening to one another."

- "Sam loves it when you overreact to his outrageous statements; he wants to get your attention."

- "The other dancers in ballet are trying really hard and feel frustrated when you correct them."

Active listening is a form of mirroring and empathy for a child's verbal communication:

- Child: "I don't want to go to music class."

- *You: "Oh, you don't want to go to music class."*

- Child: "It's not fair. How come Johnny gets to have iPad time?"

- *You: "You don't think it's fair that Johnny gets to play on his iPad and you have to wait."*

- Child: "You are the worst teacher ever!"

- *You: "You think I'm the worst right now. I hear you."*

Reflect all the micro decisions your child makes all day to reinforce awareness and confidence in self-determination:

- "You decided to try the hardest problem first."

- "You chose to take a break. What a powerful decision."

- "You decided to insult your classmate after she bumped into you."

- "First, you refused to cooperate but then you changed your mind … great cooperation."

- "I noticed that you kept trying even when the work got hard … awesome perseverance."

The **Simple Reflection** described above is very straightforward. See it, hear it, say it, and validate that moment for your child.

Complex Reflection is needed for tougher times. It gets harder to reflect a child's behavior when it is off-putting, disruptive, and inappropriate. It may trigger your urge to correct or you may get sucked into a power struggle. Watch out. During difficult moments, offer complex reflection. Translate emotion that is acted out in behavior (tip of the iceberg) into reflective **empathic translation comments** (beneath the surface). Children act out their emotions, and when they say rude or hostile statements, there is always a reason. Undesirable behavior is simultaneously a smoke signal (asking for help) and a smoke screen (a distraction obfuscating the hidden trigger).

Either way, if you react punitively or angrily to the surface behavior, the child with SECCs doesn't learn anything about coping. She perceives your comments as punitive and judgmental and becomes defensive. Reflecting the surface behavior maintains—and strengthens—power struggles. You may recognize the familiar feeling of bracing for a gladiator match of wills. You get pushed into the use of more and more forceful conversations or punishments, which break down the trust between you and your child. Translate the child's inner, underlying trigger into the reflection rather than adhering to behavioral reflection.

Instead of getting stuck commenting on outrageous, inappropriate surface behavior, mirror the feeling beneath the words, behavior, and attitude. Empathic translation comments help the child better understand what is happening inside her so she can begin problem solving:

- [Child growls and slams down pencil]

- *You: "You look stressed."*

- [Child glares when you offer a helpful tip]

- *You: "You sometimes sound angry when I try to help you."*

- [Child says something disrespectful to you]

- *You: "You don't like what I'm telling you."*

- [Child refuses to clean up when asked]

- *You: "Looks like it's hard for you to clean up today. What's stopping you?"*

Proactively set realistic and accurate expectations. When your child acts resistant, angry, or disrespectful, it is about the child. Behavior projects outward what the child is experiencing internally. These comments are likely not about you. You are the most effective social coach when you remember that behavior communicates what's going on inside the child. Adopt this powerful mindset and use your strong will to stop taking things personally.

In social-coping skills training, don't make it about you. Don't get triggered into thinking this is personal. Certainly, a rude comment or an oppositional behavior can be infuriating. If you react on a behavioral level ("You're in trouble young lady."), you and the child stay in an unresolved power struggle. If you reflect the hidden feelings beneath surface behaviors, then healing, connection, effective social coaching, and problem solving begin.

The Child-Centered View on Changing Feelings and Behavior

Coercion versus meeting the child where she is: The child-centered individual knows that you can't force anyone to do anything. You can suggest, influence, and ask. You can teach, assign, and praise. Ultimately, the child does what she chooses to do, whether positive or negative. It is so easy to get sucked into power struggles when trying to obtain cooperation. You can try to punish, dominate, or "force" a controlling (oppositional) child to comply. In the unlikely chance that you gain compliance that instance, you probably also breed hostility. The child may grudgingly do your desired task, while grumbling hateful, hostile words under her breath. You may think "I won that one. Whew." The truth is that your relationship will be worse for wear. Your child will anticipate that your next interaction will be just as awful and fractious. She will automatically begin your next chat in a closed and defensive posture.

Please evaluate the three following analogous statements based on the aphorism, "You can lead a horse to water, but you can't make it drink."

1. You could place a rope around the horse's neck and pull with all your might. It won't budge—just dig in its hooves and refuse.

2. You can move behind the horse and shove it or poke it with a needle. It won't budge, and you are likely to get kicked for your effort. Or …

3. You can stand patiently next to the horse, compassionately and affectionately pat its neck and observe. As soon as it is ready, the horse walks comfortably to the water, and you are a caring, praiseful witness to its process.

Which one of these three alternatives sounds the most pleasant? Which one sounds the most success oriented? If you choose option 3, you will witness your horse walk to the water exactly when it is ready, and you can whisper happy praise along the way. Witness its relaxed joy as it laps up the refreshing water. The person-centered trainer chooses to engage with people through the philosophy of number 3.

I know what you are thinking. "Mike, are you telling me that I have to let my child do whatever she wants?" Try not to read option 3 in such literal terms. Obviously, certain tasks or chores must be accomplished. Your child must go to bed at bedtime. She must go to science class with the rest of the students and not whenever the mood strikes. Behaviors such as refusal and defiance are unacceptable. We will get to those behaviors later in this book. Many parents who grew up in a family that valued the "pull yourself up by your bootstraps" mentality push back at the idea of child-centered reflection. It triggers their resistance and fear that they would be "letting" the child do whatever she wants. But there is an artful and more nuanced way to help children cope and succeed in the world than the coercion and control model.

The child-centered orientation to personal growth flips the traditional expectation that "wise adults will direct the child to the desired mature outcome." It takes a big-picture view and trusts that brain growth and maturation is always occurring in young people. In my clinical experience, directive or over-controlling adults sometimes exacerbate challenges and get in the way of the natural unfolding of a child's growth. Be wary of sticking to only one approach—the one you know.

We are all products of our own childhoods. You tend to give care to your child in parallel or in contrast to your parents' styles. If you feel as though your parents' style worked for you, you probably use it. If you didn't like your parents' approach to caregiving, you probably rebounded the other way and use opposite approaches. Regardless of the family you grew up in, children with SECCs need something different than traditional parenting. Traditional parenting/caregiving approaches don't always achieve the results you are looking for in terms of shaping behavior or encouraging the practice and adoption of positive social-coping skills. You might even create more tension and acting out than you prevent.

Children thrive when we observe their internal processes and allow them to blossom at their own rate. Try employing the **Now and Later Formula** and the **Culture of Readiness** to decrease power struggles and increase your child's sense of self-determination. You can provide your child a sense of (developmentally appropriate) control and responsibility with these simple techniques.

The Now and Later Formula is useful for children who get upset easily and wallow in their upset feelings. It reassures; it decreases power struggles and distress. Our clients and campers seem to feel as though whatever they are going through, it seems all encompassing and eternal. They confuse fleeting states of being with lasting traits and conditions: "I'll never finish this homework." "This is the worst day ever." "My life stinks." In these moments, the child with SECCs has a hard time envisioning the future. Like a camera, she has zoomed in on this moment. She can't calmly say, "This, too shall pass." Or "In the grand scheme of things, it isn't a big deal." She has a hard time zooming out her focus to the bigger picture that would allow her to take perspective of this challenge. And so she suffers. Your heart bleeds for your child and you strongly wish she didn't have to go through the pain and unnecessary overreaction. In that moment, neither you nor I can take away the pain. Your child is convinced that the upset, the outrage, or the task will last forever, and she will never have fun again.

Use the Now and Later Formula to reframe the moment (with empathy) that everything is temporary and a process. The Now and Later Formula uses simple language that conveys that most (if not all) experiences are a path to something else. Use this formula to compare and contrast what the child is experiencing temporarily now with the future that she has yet to imagine:

- **Right now,** you really don't want to write in your journal. **Right now,** it's hard.

- You are so overwhelmed by this assignment **right now**. Maybe when you settle down, **later,** you will be able to break it down into smaller chunks.

- **Right now,** you are upset and too angry to talk. I will be happy to speak with you about this **later**, when you are calm again.

- Your feelings are hurt **right now** by what she said—and rightfully so. **Later**, the upset will lessen, and we can make a **plan for tomorrow**.

- **This second**, you think that Johnny is a jerk for beating you at Uno. **Maybe later,** you will be in the mood to try and play Uno with him again.

The child-centered approach beautifully supports children, who, for a variety of reasons, are slow or reluctant to do things. Children may be reluctant to participate because an activity is non-preferred or new. Children may also resist instructions due to performance anxiety or out of fear that they may encounter overwhelming sensory experiences. Children who are slow processors have difficulty shifting focus or have a high need for self-control (oppositional) also may have a hard time transitioning to or initiating tasks.

For this type of child, firmer, louder or more forceful direction backfires. You may have encountered the child who does not respond to offers of rewards, consequences, playful requests, or other inducements to comply. She may shut down or argue back if you increase the force of your demand. Yelling or punishing gets you nowhere. Oppositional kids get angry and more defiant, and anxious kids feel more threatened and overwhelmed. This child frustrates you, because she makes you feel helpless and ineffectual, yet she requires clear expectations and guidance. There is a real art to engaging this child.

The child-centered antidote to this stalemate is to create a culture of readiness. Don't overreact in a punitive, impatient, or frustrated way if a child doesn't perform a behavior you desire or expect. Instead, reframe the delayed or non-performance in terms of your child *getting ready* to change states, to initiate a behavior:

- [In the midst of homework] "I see you are not ready to start working on your next subject. Maybe after a little break you will be ready."

- [Doing schoolwork] "You are thinking of an idea … you are getting ready to write."

- [Upset] "You are not ready to come out of your spot under the table. You are so upset. I know that you will come out as soon as you are ready." (Then practice patience while the child "gets ready" to come out—like the horse-to-water solution.)

- "You are not ready to talk to Sarah about your argument. I wonder when you will be ready? Maybe in a few days, or a few weeks, or longer? I know you'll decide at exactly the best time."

Notice what this subtle linguistic trick achieves. When you reflect the child's non-behavior with "You're not ready," you:

- Validate the child's internal state. She feels understood and respected.

- Disarm the child's expectation that you are going to pressure or coerce.

- Allow the child a moment to process the task or request at hand and transition her mind to perform it.

- Kindly and indirectly remind the child of your request.

Regard the benefit of following up with the focus on future readiness. When you toggle from "You're not ready now" to "Maybe you'll be ready later," you plant a seed of transition in the child's mind. You stealthily insert a hypnotic suggestion that the desired expectation is certain to be accomplished; it's only a matter of time when it will happen.

For the oppositional or avoidant child, the perception of being forced to cooperate or pushed to comply quickly feels like an external threat. It alerts their fight-flight-freeze instinct. In this somewhat indirect approach, the adult maintains her authority and the child has space to cooperate while maintaining her own sense of integrity and control.

And so, we are patient. As soon as a child is finally ready to do X, Y, or Z, we reinforce the newly revealed behavior with Targeted Positive Reflection, and potentially, reinforcement (both of which will be discussed later). When facilitated in a child-centered relationship, a child's growth and development feels very organic.

'A Work in Progress': Child-Centered Skill-Building Orientation

Accepting children's imperfections and remembering that they are incompletely formed people is vital. No child has an adult's mental abilities, and it is our job to keep that in mind. Like you or me, they are doing their best with what they have, and when they don't comply or cooperate, it's because there is a problem. When we reframe children's social behavior in a child-centered, coaching, and developmental model, we view social slips, mean comments, and conflicts exactly as they are: mistakes. They are moments when the child couldn't execute timely, desired behaviors. An obstacle, internal or external, prevented the child from performing at that moment.

Is there anything that would have helped the child execute an effective social-coping behavior? Did the child need an awareness or skill that she hadn't yet developed? Did the child have strong emotions and impulses that directed her behavior in an obtuse angle that didn't meet the situational needs? Was there something about the environment that was overwhelming for the child's sensory or emotional system and caused the miscue? The next chapter will prepare you to coach your child through emotional obstacles.

These are teachable moments. Imagine you are the coach of a team. Your child just made an error that impeded your team. What do you do? What would the best coach do? That mistake should be treated as such and should be seen as an opportunity for skill building. Every meltdown or social miscue is the child's way of saying, "I need help with this." The rest of this book provides you the skills to be the best social-emotional coach you can be. Go team.

CHAPTER 2

SUPPORTING SELF-REGULATION IN SOCIAL-COPING SKILLS TRAINING

Imagine you are sailing a mighty ocean liner. You are the captain of your ship and confidently hold the steering wheel in one hand and the throttle in the other. You have a telescope and with it, you see an iceberg ahead. The white cap juts out of the water. Experienced captain that you are, you also know that beneath the surface of the water there is likely to be a wider and deeper piece of ice that could sink your ship. Wisely, you plot a new course for safety and success. If you don't change course, you are certain to collide with the iceberg and sink. Everyone will be in peril.

The Iceberg Theory of Emotion and Behavior

Children's behavior is much like the iceberg. The child's visible and audible behavior, like the ice cap above the surface, is obvious and concrete. You can see and hear it. Like the rest of us, you have reactions to behaviors you see. You like some, dislike others, find some endearing, and judge others to be horrible. Behaviors you witness trigger memories and emotions in you. They sometimes cause you to react in habitual ways based on years of experience. Other behaviors you witness cause your mind to lurch forward to the future, imagining victories or fearing repercussions.

As captain, you need to stay in the now and keep your mind focused on the present interaction. Distraction or overreaction can mean disaster for your crew. The surface of the iceberg that you see alerts you that something is going on. After reading this book, you will be able to use the Iceberg Theory to steer your responses to your child's behavior by considering: "What's beneath the surface of the behavior?" "What is the wisdom of the behavior?" "What is the behavior telling me he needs?" The Iceberg Theory guides your responses and interventions to be supportive and thoughtful.

If the surface of the iceberg represents the overt behaviors you can see and hear, beneath the surface of a behavior lies its hidden motivation, also known as its **trigger**. Every behavior is caused by feelings, tensions, sensory experiences, memories, expectations, hunger, sleepiness, and many other internal experiences. The behavior, like the ice cap, is a signal to explore the possible triggers beneath the surface. This is the **wisdom of the behavior**. Each behavior is trying to tell us something about your child's needs. To tap into the wisdom of the behavior, you must ask: "What is this behavior trying to tell me?" Then, respond in a strategic and planned manner.

As captain of the ship, if you over-focus on the surface ice cap you will misjudge the size and shape of the danger below the water, and your ship may be damaged. If you react exclusively to your child's surface actions (behavior) without acknowledging the trigger below, you will most likely find yourself trapped in a cycle of power struggle, conflict, hurt feelings, and disconnection. People are not robots, and too much focus on behavior grinds a child's spirit.

Additionally, when you react to surface behavior, there is no doubt your child feels your displeasure. However, will he learn better ways to behave when you call out his behavior? Will he acquire new social skills when you correct him? It is human nature for us to react to the behaviors we see in others. However, in social-coping skills training with children with SECCs, you may be treading water or sinking if you keep running into that iceberg.

Use this concept with your child. Introduce it with the iceberg image, and then repeatedly ask your child, "What was beneath the surface?" "What were you thinking when you did 'X?'" "What were you feeling when you did 'Y?'" "Was something hard going on when you did 'Z?'" Help your child develop self-awareness, the ability to identify triggers to his behavior, and eventually, the ability to anticipate and steer clear of obstacles.

In no way am I suggesting that you only explore issues beneath the surface. Remember, this book adheres to the Philosophy of *AND*. One complaint about therapists is that they analyze everything. We must look at the entire iceberg, top and bottom. When you include this beneath-the-surface method of looking at behavior, you become part of a long-term solution. What triggers contributed to this unhelpful behavior? Was it something stressful about the environment that we can change? Is my child repeatedly shutting down in gym class? What's going on there? Being curious about triggers beneath the surface of the iceberg enable you to offer social coaching, accommodate the environment, tweak the reward/consequence system, and insightfully collaborate with other caregivers in your child's success.

The Iceberg Theory

=Behavior=

thoughts feelings

wants needs

sensory tension

2.5 MAIN MOTIVATIONS

① ↑ Fun and Pleasure

② ↓ Discomfort, stress, pain

③ Power, control

Beneath the Surface: The Two-and-a-Half Main Motivations for Behavior

Sometimes children's behavior seems confusing. Self-sabotaging behavior "cuts off his nose to spite his face." Exasperated parents and educators with whom I have consulted often ask, "Why did he do that?" Let's over-simplify briefly to gain clarity (we can always think in more nuanced terms later). For our purposes, human motivation can be boiled down into two (and a half) main forces:

1. The drive to *Increase Pleasure or Comfort* includes gaining attention, mental/physical stimulation, good feelings, sense of play

2. The drive to *Decrease Stress or Discomfort* involves escaping bodily tension/frustration, ameliorating uncomfortable or overwhelming feelings and pain

3. The "half" is the drive for *Control and Power*, which actually falls in both numbers one and two. **Oppositional Behavior** reveals the child's beneath-the-surface motivation to over-control his internal and external world. Refusing directives and requests, the word "No." is the child's instinctive correction to feeling out of control. The child gains both pleasure and relief from discomfort by forcing continuation of pleasurable activities or by refusing to do things that cause frustration and discomfort.

You may ask, "So what? What's the benefit of knowing basic motivation? You can use this to understand why a child seemingly chooses to perform inappropriate or ineffective behaviors. Consider the fact that the child is driven by the two (and a half) motivations above, and then funnel that through the lens of the child who doesn't intuitively understand the unwritten rules of socialization. Take a minute to try to use our motivators to better understand these behaviors:

*   6-year-old Johnny stands on his desk and pulls his pants down in the middle of class. Is he gaining anything? Pleasure? Attention? Is he avoiding discomfort? Getting out of a task or environment? Is he exerting control? Some combination of the three?

*   11-year-old Martina complains that she is lonely but pulls out a book and reads on the bench every day instead of joining her friends at recess. Is she seeking pleasure? What possible discomfort might she be avoiding? Is this an example of exerting control? Some combination of the three?

*   13-year-old Daniel refuses to wear a winter jacket on the coldest day of the year and has a tantrum over his parent's demand. Is he seeking pleasure? Avoiding discomfort? Exerting control? Some combination of the three?

*   17-year-old Garrett argues and debates the family rule of "no smartphones in your bedroom or bathroom." He repeatedly sneaks it to his bedroom and is given consequences. Seeking pleasure? Avoiding discomfort? Exerting control? Some combination of the three? List all the possibilities.

The tip-of-the-iceberg response is to judge the behaviors as good or bad, and to communicate your reaction. You might instinctively roll your eyes, lecture, or assign a consequence. Using our two (and a half) motivations, what new questions would you ask the child in each of these situations? In what ways would the conversation differ now that you have some educated guesses about why the behavior took place?

To assess if the child was seeking pleasure, you might ask, "Do you get anything good out of doing that?" "Tell me what you were thinking when you chose to do that." Or "Does doing that make you feel good?"

To assess if the child was avoiding or escaping discomfort, ask, "Is there anything hard/scary/ uncomfortable about ____[what's going on]____?" Or "Is there a part of you that wants to avoid/ doesn't want to deal with _____?"

It's a bit harder to simply ask a child if he is seeking control, but in many ways, controlling behavior is self-evident. During a time of peace, you can approach your child and ask about the controlling behavior. "Hey Daniel, remember two days ago when you didn't want to wear your jacket when it was minus five degrees wind chill? What was so bad about wearing it? Tell me all the reasons. Was one part of it that you just wanted to do it your way?"

Emotional GPS: A Framework to Effectively Navigate and Support Children's Emotional States

Triggers lie beneath the surface of the iceberg. When something occurs in the child's world, even something small, it can activate the submerged trigger, which then surges to the surface. The unhelpful behavior displayed at the tip of the iceberg lets you know to look for the trigger. The number-one driver of impulses and behavior in children is emotional **arousal**.

The simplest definition for arousal is the level of the child's self-regulation, mental activity, emotion, and physical energy. Arousal is the term for the degree of mental activation, alertness, and emotional reactivity a child experiences in relation to the environment. Frustration, excitement, anxiety, and hyperactivity all are powerful triggers beneath the iceberg's surface that may rev a child up and cause unhelpful behaviors.

Many children who struggle socially and emotionally have a rough time identifying their emotional and arousal states. They become overwhelmed. This causes iceberg behaviors such as flash anger or tantrums, refusal to try new things, running away to hide, running around being hyper-silly, and bothering others. There is a continuum of arousal and frustration, ranging from low to high levels. One little known feature of high levels of dysregulation (tantrums, panic attacks, running away/eloping, shutting down) is that the individual loses much of his rational thinking and receptive or expressive language ability. In short, the child becomes irrational, unreasonable, and has a hard time processing language and using words to communicate effectively.

Most children and adults don't know quite how to measure their levels of arousal. Who thinks about these things? You need to when you live or work with a dysregulated person. Until they are taught to do so, children with SECCs generally are not aware in real time of their level of frustration or their emotions, which makes it hard for them to select effective coping strategies. Additionally, parents and caregivers report to me that they don't know the best way to respond to behaviors at various levels of emotion and arousal.

When caregivers mismatch their support strategy with the child's level of frustration, they may accidentally contribute to the very tantrum they hoped to avoid. Wouldn't it be great if we had something to guide our support strategies?

I created a visual framework to do just that. Using colors and a ten-point rating scale, this framework provides a shared visual language for children and caregivers to talk about the child's levels of frustration. Like a GPS app on your smartphone, our visual framework provides step-by-step directions to your desired destination—self-regulation. It creates an accurate and shared awareness of the child's states of arousal. Our GPS enables kids to select and use realistic strategies for each level of frustration/arousal. The framework empowers you to employ appropriate support strategies for each level as well. We call the framework **Emotional GPS**, a structured thought process that guides children's coping tasks and caregivers' support efforts. We use four colors and assign them increasing numbers to depict four levels of arousal, Purple (1-3), Yellow (4-6), Orange (7-9), and Red (10).

In the calmer Purple and Yellow phases, you can use **facilitative techniques** that empower the child to make decisions and to use existing social-coping skills. In the more intense phases of arousal, Orange and Red, the child's mental flexibility and language are less available, and the adult offers increasing structure through limited acceptable choices, **directive techniques**. Both your child and you have specific tasks and roles at each level:

Purple Phase—Your child is calm, relaxed, and focused. He can talk, have fun, learn, plan, and problem solve to the best of his ability. He has access to his best language and thinking skills. It's his best self.

The child for whom self-regulation is difficult is relieved to finally be feeling good in the Purple Phase. He wishes the good vibes could go on forever and is shocked when something goes wrong. Perhaps he has a disagreement with a peer, or a caregiver gives instructions to stop a preferred activity to transition to a new task. We coach our clients and campers to enjoy the Purple Phase, but to be ready for anything. Have your flexibility and compromise at the ready to protect your Purple Phase.

Children's tasks in the Purple Phase:

- Enjoy. Learn and play.

- Don't be shocked if something doesn't go your way; stay ready to problem solve and negotiate

- Keep your "bendiness" (flexibility) and be ready to "Change your mind on purpose."

Caregivers' Purple Phase role is to facilitate and reinforce:

- Give targeted praise to reinforce the child's positive decisions that initiate and sustain the Purple Phase

- Use **"Jeopardy Coaching"** (in chapter four): ask facilitating questions as often as possible. "How do you want to handle this?" "What do you want to do about that?"

Yellow Phase—Something has just gone wrong and the child experiences a bit of stress. Perhaps a peer does or says something he doesn't like. Maybe there is a disagreement. A parent just instructed the child to do something un-preferred. The child experiences the first, lower levels of tension and frustration. Many children don't recognize this is happening and don't realize it is a perfect opportunity to nip things in the bud and problem solve.

Fortunately, the child retains most of his cognitive functioning and language in Yellow. His existing coping skills are still available, and he can problem solve to the best of his ability. If the child is an independent problem solver, he can probably handle the situation. Children who are dependent problem solvers are still calm enough to use adult support in this phase. If the child is in social-coping skills therapy, his learned coping skills can help. In the Yellow Phase, children are calm enough and possess enough of their cognitive capability to benefit from adult coaching.

Children's tasks:

- Use words (language) to let others know how they feel or what they need

  o "I feel _____."

  o "I want _____."

  o "I'd like _____."

- Use social-coping skills to stay calm enough to solve problems, negotiate, compromise, and practice flexibility.

Caregivers' Yellow Phase role:

- Use open-ended "Jeopardy Coaching" facilitative questions as often as possible to encourage the child's independent coping-thinking. "How do you want to handle this?" "What do you want to do about that?"

- Use specific "Jeopardy Coaching" facilitative questions to trigger the child's memory of learned social-coping skills: "What might work here: your Dino Technique or Rescue Thoughts?" "You're near the cliff. Is there a rescue thought for this situation?" "Is anyone losing a pinky finger here? How big a deal is this?" "Can you be bendy/flexible about this?" (These are all catch phrases from frustration tolerance coping skills lessons in the Art of Friendship Social-Coping Curriculum that will appear in subsequent books.)

- Give **Targeted Positive Reflection** (a.k.a. **TPR**, in chapter three) to reinforce the child's successful coping with the frustration.

Orange Phase—Low-level stress rises to *distress*. The child is now showing physical signs of significant frustration such as clenching fists, stomping, grunting, or grabbing his head. At this point, the child is beginning to lose mental flexibility, problem-solving, and language ability. The receptive language centers of the brain constrict. Your open-ended support and a lot of talking only escalates the child's frustration. He needs more clarity, direction, and structure, with minimal language; but he can still handle making a simple choice. The desperate, compassionate goal here is to avoid further escalation to the disastrous Red Phase.

Children's tasks:

- Let an adult know what the problem is and what the child wants

- Choose one of two acceptable coping strategies to decrease emotional arousal to return to the Yellow Phase for problem solving

- Take a break or solve the problem

Your Orange Phase role:

- Temporarily relax the expectation, request, or time deadline. Decrease the urgency or speed of the situation so the child doesn't feel trapped. "Hold on a second, I'm not saying you have to do _____ right now. Let's just take a breath and regroup."

- Decrease the load on the child's language-processing center by being extremely brief (no lectures).

- Offer an **acceptable choice**. Increase structure and decrease demand on the child's flexibility and executive functioning. "Acceptable choices" offer the child two concrete success-oriented options:

  o   "Do you want to use "X" coping strategy or "Y" coping strategy?"

  o   "You can take a break, or you can solve this. What sounds better right now?"

  o   "You can calm down here or you can escape to a calming-down spot."

Notice that whatever the child chooses will work, and you won't have made matters more complicated with too much talking, too much pressure or too much choice. We want to give the child every chance to avoid a complete loss of control, the Red Phase.

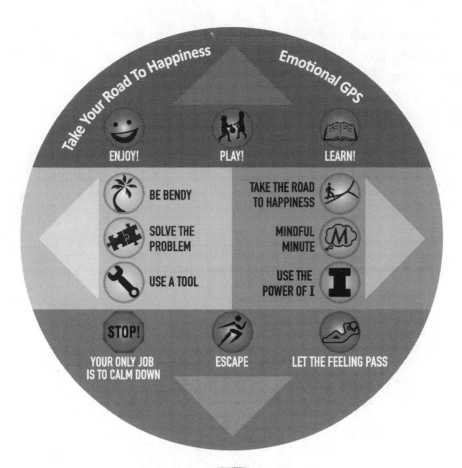

Take Your Road To Happiness — **Emotional GPS**

ENJOY!   PLAY!   LEARN!

BE BENDY
SOLVE THE PROBLEM
USE A TOOL

TAKE THE ROAD TO HAPPINESS
MINDFUL MINUTE
USE THE POWER OF I

STOP!
YOUR ONLY JOB IS TO CALM DOWN

ESCAPE

LET THE FEELING PASS

Take Your Road To Happiness

MY BEST TOOLS:

1. _____

2. _____

3. _____

4. _____

PROBLEM SOLVING:

1. State the problem:

_____

2. List 2-3 solutions:

a. _____

b. _____

c. _____

3. Pick 1 to try!

4. If it works - congrats!
   If not, go to #3

STOP!

MY CALMING PLAN:

_____

_____

Red Phase—At this point, your child has lost self-control and self-regulation. The brain's limbic system (**"Dino Brain"**) hijacks your child's cognition, causing a loss of reason and language processing. Your child can barely tolerate any talking from you. Sometimes eye contact can intensify or prolong the meltdown. The fight, flight, or freeze mechanism kicks in with rage, physical or verbal aggression, running around, elopement, or wild silliness.

The Red Phase is a wave of intense energy much like a tidal wave. Once started, the Red Wave can't be stopped short with a consequence or a clever strategy. It must crest, crash on shore, and then recede. It always does, and your child always recovers. Our task moving forward is to help create a compassionate response with the reassuring expectation that it is temporary. Your child always survives it and does return to his regulated state.

In the Red Phase, your child has regressed developmentally to 2- to 4-year-old levels of functioning. You can't reason with a tantruming 2- to 4-year-old, so don't try to do it with your Red Phase child. The child is no longer a candidate for any of the cognitive and skill-based strategies he has learned. He is like a raging dinosaur and his only job is to calm down. Stop lecturing or discussing it or else you will make it worse. You can escalate or prolong the Red Wave or you can allow it to run its shortest possible course. Your role is crucial.

There is only one thing for the child to do, and there is only one thing for you to do. Say, "Your only job is to calm down. I'll be over here." In fact, at this point, your child's only task is to allow the wave of energy to crash and recede.

This is extremely intense for the caregiver, and you may find that your breathing and heartrate accelerate. You feel angry yourself or want to argue back. Your child says the most disrespectful things. (Remember, language skills and reason dramatically decrease, but the mouth still works like an unguided missile system.)

While the child is possessed by his Dino Brain, don't take anything personally. When the meltdown switch has been flipped on, what should children and caregivers do?

Children's Red Phase tasks:

- Calm Down. Period. Nothing else. This is the child's only task, because nothing productive happens when he is unreasonable and minimally processing language.

Your Red Phase tasks:

- Proactively, during a time of peace, identify a calming spot and materials with the child collaboratively; provide calming toys, books, markers, or fidgets (depending on the child). I don't guarantee that the child will go to the calming spot every time, but it can be an important part of a Red Phase Strategy to pre-select a good place for the child to rage out the Red Wave.

- Keep everyone safe. Escort your child out of a dangerous or social situation if possible. "C'mon, let's go." You may place an arm around his back or lightly hold a wrist to direct him to walk to safety. If your child freezes in place and refuses to move, you may need to clear the room of siblings or classmates, instead.

- Use minimal language and minimal talking.

- Try to get the child to a calming-down spot, if he is willing to move.

- Get down on child's level; firmly say: "Your only job is to calm down. I'll be over here," then give him space.

- Some children respond well if, while you say that, you hold their hands together in front of them. A light squeeze on forearms (strategic, not out of anger) sometimes helps to focus your child's attention for your quick statement. As soon as you say, "I'll be over here," let go of his hands and back off by at least five feet.

- Now you must breathe deeply and wait patiently for the wave to crash and recede

- Know your child. If touch will escalate a meltdown, don't do it. Likewise, don't stare at your melting-down child. Your eye contact may be perceived as threatening when the fight-flight-freeze Dino Brain is raging and you might exacerbate it. Look away. If you need to maintain supervision of the child, look three-to-five feet to the left or right of the child and use your peripheral vision to keep him safe.

- Breathe slowly and deeply so you stay calm and don't pick up the child's racing, intense pace. You can help yourself remain calm by reminding yourself that you are having a perfectly fine day, that these are the child's emotions. Separate your feelings from the child's and model slow, deep, calming breaths.

- Ignore all insults or wild comments; this is Dino Brain testing and manipulation designed to suck you in and prolong the Red Phase.

- Wait out the meltdown, and as soon as the child is fully calm, offer heaps of Targeted Positive Reflection: "Great job calming down. You beat your record of thirty-three minutes. Let's see if you can break your calm-down record next time." This is the payoff for your compassionate support of the Red Phase. Your child discovers that *he* is the one who calms himself down. *He* does it. You don't represent the calming factor; you are the witness to the child's process. Your message is, "*You* always calm down; *you* can develop confidence that when you get overwhelmed, it is never permanent. *You* are resilient and can get back to fun/school/work."

When is Behavior *Misbehavior* and When is It Red Phase Loss of Control?

Children may say mean things to each other at times. They may be disrespectful to adults if they feel uncomfortable or misunderstood. There are plenty of childhood behaviors that are not okay: refusing to share, hitting. and exclusion, for example. As we progress further into this book, we will cover ways to discourage and decrease unacceptable behavior.

When discussing arousal and Emotional GPS, we must *separate behavior miscues* and *misbehavior* from Red Phase actions. In Purple, Yellow, and Orange phases the child retains some or all his self-control. Things your child says and does are motive-based and at least partially intended behaviors. You can also chalk those missteps up to SECCs. The child lacks the social skills to execute desired social behaviors.

In the Red Phase, however, the child has lost all control. Behaviors that occur when the child is completely disinhibited are some of the worst and scariest we may see and hear. Children shout curses at parents. "You are the worst parent ever. I hate you." They may destroy property. I have personally witnessed children punching parents in the stomach and kicking babysitters' legs. Once, an enraged camper tried to bend my fingers backwards as if to rip them off. Red Phase behaviors are completely out of the child's control at that point. It is also out of character. The Red Phase child is a completely different person than when he is in the other functional phases of the Emotional GPS. He loses all reason, and the fight-flight-freeze center of his brain—the same one that dinosaurs and lizards have—takes control.

In my clinical opinion and in my programs, we do not punish or shame a child for Red Phase of loss of control. The loss of control is not willful—although sometimes it may look that way. No one wants to lose control. Your child did not wake up this morning thinking, "At 4:45 I plan on having the mother of all tantrums." It's laughable to think so.

Your child hates losing control. It feels rotten. He feels embarrassed and bad about himself. Punishment does not teach him anything in this phase. Likewise, lecturing and other guilt-inducing conversations produce no improvement. It is okay to let the child know the impact of the tantrum on the class, family, or relationship—after he completely calms down.

Destructive and hurtful comments after the meltdown should not be punished, however. A realistic logical consequence after a meltdown could be to have the child help clean up and make amends when possible. I am not a huge fan of forcing anyone to say, "I'm sorry." A resentful and passive-aggressive, forced "Sorry" makes the aggressor resent the victim all over again. It is meaningless. I find it is more effective to reflect the impact of the aggression and, in question form, see if the child wants to apologize, "You really hurt your friend's feelings when you were screaming at him when you were in the Red Phase. He might be a little scared to be around you after that. *Is there anything you might say to him that might help him feel better?*" This is facilitative social coaching versus a forced apology. Lastly, after the child returns fully to Purple Phase, it is important to review the trigger to the meltdown. Collaboratively, you can develop a coping plan to prevent a meltdown in similar future situations (see the discussion about social coaching and the Think-Feel-Do Problem Solving Worksheet in chapter four).

So, the Red Phase is non-functional and out of control. Behaviors in that phase really aren't the child's fault. However, children must be held accountable for behaviors in the Purple Phase, Yellow Phase, and Orange Phase. There, you can use all the strategies found in this book. Social-coping skills instruction, social coaching, and behavior shaping through rewards and consequences, should happen in the three functional phases. The Red Phase receives only compassion and guidance to calm down. We need to help children develop a safety plan, carving out space to more rapidly calm and recover post-meltdown. Once the Red Phase plan is created, most of therapy should focus on proactive preventive coping skills to decrease or even eliminate Red Phase loss of control.

Differentiating Between Desired 'Increase-Behaviors' vs. 'Decrease-Behaviors'

All functional behaviors are not created the same, and different undesired behaviors require different responses. Thomas W. Phelan, Ph.D., author of the classic parenting book *1-2-3 Magic* contributed a clear and valuable distinction between types of behaviors. He identified:

- "Start Behaviors" are those things you want the child to start doing—or do more of. I call them **Increase-Behaviors.** It is critical that all caregivers know that Increase-Behaviors *are not created through consequences or punishment.* Consequences and punishment squelch behaviors. The Art of Friendship perspective is that Increase-Behaviors are developed by first teaching positive replacement social-coping skills, and then implementing positive feedback cycles (to be discussed in chapter three). Our program strives to elicit more and more positive replacement skills and behaviors; we improve social competence and emotional coping. Old unhelpful/undesired behaviors fade away when kids learn and practice new positive social-coping skills.

- Phelan identified Stop-Behaviors as those you want the child to STOP doing or do less of. I call these **Decrease-Behaviors**. The behaviors you want to decrease or extinguish require ignoring or negative reinforcement in the form of predictable limits and logical consequences. Limit setting will be discussed more thoroughly in chapter 5.

Everyone hopes for inappropriate and disruptive behavior to stop. Our greatest wish is for the child with SECCs to be able to join in socially and succeed in the classroom and beyond. Often, when a child makes a social or behavioral miscue, the adult instinct is to respond with lectures explaining why it was wrong or by giving consequences. The underlying logic holds that "punishment" (negative consequences) dissuades kids from misbehaving. There is certainly a rightful place for negative consequences, and we will cover them later. But for children with SECCs, frustrated lectures or your emotional outbursts can be shaming and adds insult to injury. Instilling more frustration in a child with SECCs will not make him any more willing to try a positive coping behavior.

Sculpting the Iceberg

Did you ever see an ice sculpture? Chain saws are used to make the overall shape of the sculpture before finer tools are used to carve the details. The sculptor works in 360 degrees around the block of ice, chiseling a bit from the front, then working around to the sides and back. It is quite a process. If you want to shape a child's behavior (the tip of his iceberg), you need to consider the whole child in 360 degrees. This includes social skills, emotional coping skills, executive functioning, and impulse control. Let's discuss the process of shaping behavior among children with SECCs.

In the case of children with SECCs, you can't simply tell or coerce the child to "Cut that out." and expect results. Why can't you give a global command? Because it's not your child's fault. Most kids with SECCs happen to be rule-followers. They have hearts of gold, wish to be successful, and would never choose to commit the same miscue over and over again. Remember, their neurology provides them with below-average intuitive thinking, self-awareness, and self-control. They struggle to learn and adapt from their mistakes. If they could simply stop, they would. Wouldn't it be great if the child knew something better to do?

Instead, the child needs direct instruction in positive replacement thoughts and skills. The Art of Friendship Social-Coping curriculum is designed to do just that. We start by using the Iceberg Theory. You see a behavior that is not working for the child, socially or emotionally. You think, "What is beneath the surface of that behavior? What does the child need here? Why couldn't my child perform the necessary task in that moment? What is the missing social or coping skill that caused it?" Then, select and teach one of the social-coping lessons to provide the child with positive replacement awareness and behaviors. Success. The child now possesses the knowledge and the skills to succeed, right? Yes and no.

The child still needs to practice and integrate the new behavior before being able to execute it consistently. This is hard. Any new behavior must replace old, ingrained habits and patterns. You should expect the child to make mistakes while practicing and implementing these new skills. Let this expectation help you generate extra patience and compassion. As we move forward, this book will describe a holistic program that lovingly and creatively instills positive replacement skills, compassionately coaches through mistakes and difficult moments, and reinforces skill development with passion and joy.

SECTION 2

SOCIAL-COPING SKILL TRAINING: LOVE WITH LIMITS

CHAPTER 3

THERAPEUTIC LOVE: CREATING POSITIVE CYCLES FOR GROWTH

The objective of this section, and the entire program, is to elicit "Increase-Behaviors" (positive replacement behaviors) by replacing negative cycles with positive cycles. We will:

- Build and reinforce social-coping skills

- Fade ineffective, undesired behavior

- Elicit cooperation and improved behaviors

Ineffective social behaviors stand out, interrupt the day, attract negative attention and hostility, and are sometimes downright inappropriate. At home and in the classroom, disruptive and Red/ Orange Zone behavior are obstacles to completion of family plans and classroom procedures. Interruptions to the family schedule and chores may be frustrating for you. As adults, we are super busy and stretched thin. We just hope to get through the day as quickly and efficiently as possible. If you're a teacher, you just want to teach and complete your lesson. When a child's behavior creates friction or obstacles, it stands out like a neon sign flashing, "Detour … Detour … "

It's human nature, and easy for us, to notice and comment on a child's negative behaviors. We comment out of our personal need to get a quick fix, to correct the undesired behavior and to get our process back on track. We overlook the good behaviors ("good" is a value judgment) because a) we expect them, b) we hope for them, and c) we are concerned with completing our multitude of daily responsibilities. And so, the child with SECCs gets corrected. A lot.

Unfortunately, frequent correction and redirection sparks a negative feedback cycle that usually restricts the teaching and learning of social-coping skills. Children perceive that they got "caught". Inevitably, constant correction and redirection lead children to infer that they are "bad kids." Being called out for behavioral errors may induce shame or embarrassment that they were off-task … again. Imagine the discouragement and tension that is created in a good-hearted child when she is redirected for the umpteenth time that day. Frequent corrections threaten the child's self-esteem and confidence, "I always mess up." "My teacher doesn't like me." "I'm not good at *anything.*"

When the caregiver provides frequent social or behavioral corrections, the child's independence is unwittingly discouraged, because the adult performs most of the social-coping thinking for the child. School-age children are supposed to develop an ever-growing sense of agency and independence. When this developmental task is thwarted by insecurity or the constant need for adult guidance, children struggle emotionally. When natural developmental sequences are blocked, children grow tense and experience strong emotions of anger, anxiety, or depression. In the face of such overpowering stress and emotion, they often develop unhealthy behaviors and coping styles. Withdrawal, blaming, oppositional (controlling), domination, or manipulative behavior are all attempts to manage the painful emotions that are created out of the child's negative feedback loop with the world.

Consider the negative cycle that emerges through no one's fault or intent. Your child's tension leads to behavioral acting out, acting out leads to adult redirection, and the redirection leads to heightened tension. It is not intentional on the part of the caring adult. The child's unhelpful or ineffective behavior seems to call for constant correction. It energizes the negative cycle. It seems to trigger future undesired behaviors and ruptures the caregiver-child relationship. Frequent correction of negative behaviors actually slows the child's acquisition of social-coping skills.

Interrupt and Reverse Negative Cycles by Focusing on Positive Social-Coping Skills and Behavior

Like a frog hopping from lily pad to lily pad to cross a pond, a child tends to grow from accomplishment to accomplishment. If the frog misses the lily pad, *plop*. It sinks into the dark water. It somehow struggles back up on the lily pad to continue its journey. Each landing is an achievement. The frog breathes a sigh of relief in recognition, "I made it." Before preparing for its next leap, Frog steadies its feet on the only firm platform around, celebrates its success to that point, and continues forward.

Achieving a new skill itself isn't the sole ingredient in child development, though. On some level, like the frog landing on the lily pad, the child must recognize, even unconsciously, the new level of success. If the child doesn't register the new platform she's on, recognition by an observant mentor amplifies the achievement.

To notice the achievement is to give it material substance. It validates it. When a young child learns to read, she first learns the letters. Encouraging and enthusiastic teachers and caregivers celebrate the success with the child. "You know your A, B, Cs." This becomes the child's new baseline skill and integrates with her identity in the statement, "*I* know my A, B, C's." From that platform, she is ready to take the next leap by learning and practicing the sound each letter makes. The cheerleaders in the child's life celebrate with her when she gives effort and succeeds, and together, they establish a new, more advanced baseline. After spending some time mastering the letter sounds, the student learns common letter-sound combinations, and finally, she can read. She experiences her own achievement, takes confidence from mastering skills at each new platform, and readies herself for the next level. Social and coping-skill development follow a similar pattern.

Let's extend the reading metaphor to situations in which a child has an obstacle to learning, like dyslexia. Learning to read is extra difficult, which makes many children feel stupid and different from typical students. The child needs very specialized teaching approaches—along with extra encouragement and reinforcement from teachers. If the dyslexic child only, or mostly, receives a feedback loop with correction, as opposed to specific learning strategies and encouragement, the child will surely suffer.

Children with SECCs have social processing differences akin to a social learning disability and benefit from a similar approach. We don't want to correct too aggressively or frequently, because the child already feels unsure and vulnerable. We should set skill-based goals, teach positive replacement skills, celebrate each little victory, and create new launch pads for the next skill.

First, check your attitude toward behavior. Remain mindful that behavioral miscues reveal gaps in social-coping skills beneath the surface. Intentionally adopt a philosophy that you and your child are in a teaching and learning process—and relationship. We hope the child learns new positive social-emotional coping skills and behaviors. The best way for her to leapfrog her way to social-emotional growth is through the creation of positive cycles. Here's how:

Positive Observation

We already established that it's human nature to notice all the little (and large) unhelpful behaviors. Commit to observing every positive behavior that your child performs. It's not very hard to do but requires a commitment to try. In two brief exercises you can begin the process of developing and strengthening the skill of **positive attention**.

First, for five minutes, observe your child playing, doing artwork, doing homework, or building something. Imagine yourself as a sports play-by-play announcer and make a running commentary of every itty-bitty decision and behavior your child does. You can do it in your head, but I suggest jotting down all the micro-decisions that your child makes, both positive and negative. It might sound like this: "She is taking paper out to draw … she's picking up big paper, no, wait … she is putting it down and changing to her origami book. She is turning to a page and looking at the directions. She is making her first fold … She doesn't like it … She crumples up the first paper and starts again … "

Each motion and behavior you see reveals a mental process of decision-making. The first time you try this exercise, it is shocking and revealing to learn just how many microscopic decisions go into the execution of any task or activity. Put down this book, grab a pen and paper, and try this exercise.

Welcome back. You now know how to observe micro-decisions and behaviors. Good start. The next step is to use your newfound observational skills to create positive cycles. Read on to learn how to supercharge your positive observations into a positive skill-building force. Here's how:

Add Targeted Positive Reflection (T.P.R.)

For many children with SECCs, self-awareness is developed later than their mainstream peers. They seem to float (or bounce) through their day committing a myriad of behaviors moment to moment, but without awareness of whether the behavior was helpful or not. Remember, many children with SECCs don't intuitively read social cues. They often miss or misread the environmental feedback that socializes neurotypical kids. For this reason, they don't know, amidst the sea of behaviors they execute all day, which are the better ones to repeat and which ones are unhelpful. How can the child learn which social skills are better to repeat and which ones to jettison?

When an adult verbally and directly reflects the child's behavior or feeling, the behavior is validated. It is reinforced by the adult's attention. To make valid means to make real. When an adult verbally points out a child's behavioral miscue, it's like taking a snapshot and validating that mess-up moment. This magnifies why negative cycles are so powerful. When you comment on negative behaviors, you make them real for the child. That's why it feels so bad. That's why she gets so hurt and defensive.

On the other hand, when you verbally reflect positive behaviors and contributions to a child, it makes *that* behavior real. The child realizes, "Oh, I just did something good. Maybe I should do that again." If the child takes those good feelings in and repeats the positive behavior once or twice, suddenly you have a positive pattern. Patterns lead to habits. This is the power of the ultra-positive social training approach we employ.

Imagine if you harness your positive attention and help your child create new launch pads for growth each day. For social-coping skills training purposes it's imperative that you learn to speak up when you notice each positive thing your child does. The next skill is to learn how to give brief, very specific verbal reflection, specifically of the positive choice the child made.

Take a second to look back at your notes from your first observation session of your child. Insert a star next to each behavior you listed that could be worthy of positive reflection. Write down what targeted praise you might say to your child for each behavior. In the next paragraph, I rewrote the notes from the first observation, inserting in italics the targeted praise I might use.

"She is taking paper out to draw *I love that you are finding something to entertain yourself.* … She's picking up big paper, no, wait … she is putting it down and changing to her origami book. *You changed your mind."* ... *She is turning to a page and looking at the directions.* **Great job stopping to check the directions. ... She is making her first fold ... She doesn't like it ... She crumples up the first paper and starts again.* **Wow. You stayed calm and tried again; that was awesome ...*

I found four things to praise in that small sequence. You can too. In my programs we call specific praise of behavior **Targeted Positive Reflection (TPR).**

TPR can be accomplished in a few ways. Please note that you never should give general, nonspecific praise like, "Great job." "You're so smart." or "You're so cute." Nonspecific praise doesn't help the child with SECCs because, as I mentioned already, it doesn't help the child differentiate which behavior was helpful or desired. Additionally, the latter two examples are states that are not in the child's control. She can't intentionally try to behave smarter or cuter by your praising those traits. General praise such as this is hollow; it doesn't contribute to self-esteem. Self-esteem and confidence grow by experiencing competence, achievement, coping, and success. For social-coping skills development, you should positively reflect concrete behavior—things you can see and hear the child do.

You can simply say what you are seeing in an enthusiastic tone:

- You changed your mind!

- You worked that out!

- You didn't give up!

- You compromised!

- You used your words!

You can also add a complimentary word or phrase to your reflection:

- Great job compromising!

- Thank you for carrying your plate to the counter!

- I like how you transitioned to bedtime tonight!

- Wonderful assertiveness! I heard you loud and clear.

- You stood up to that bully; you are powerful!

It is helpful to vary your language, so you don't say "Great job doing _____" over and over. You don't want to sound like a praise robot.

Let's do another observation exercise to power up your observational and reflective powers. Observe your child again for five minutes. This time think of and jot down a targeted positive reflection of each positive behavior or decision your child makes during this period. Put down the book and give this a try.

I know that this is a different way of seeing the world and speaking than you are used to. It will feel artificial, forced, and awkward at first. Starting something meaningful and new requires your own decision and a commitment to practice. You are on your own lily pad path with this, and I believe in you. In a relatively short time, TPR will flow off your lips easily. Repeat this exercise until you begin feeling more comfortable with Targeted Positive Reflection.

There is a side benefit to practicing TPR. You may notice that you will do less police work and crowd control among all your children or students. If you teach or have a family with multiple children, you can give TPR to the other children or students who *are* on task. Remember that repeated redirection grinds down children with SECCs. Additionally, it can be used for everyone in your family or classroom (kids, adults, and even your parents.). Everyone responds well to positive reflection. It turns out, all of us want our goodness to be noticed and validated. Imagine if everyone in the whole world spoke to one another this way.

Let's play with the following school scenario to reinforce TPR. Max, the child with SECCs, wanders away from his desk and into the cubby area in the classroom. Start TPRing other kids: "I see Emily, Sam, and Benjamin all sitting quietly waiting for directions … I see Daniel and Phoebe heading to their seats …" Max hears this indirect cuing and reroutes himself toward his seat—just what you want. Individualize your TPR to Max: "Max, great thinking. You brought your body back to the group. What a great decision."

Notice all the benefits for Max: you avoided the direct correction, enabled Max to think independently about the social expectations, and select an appropriate behavior to comply and fit in. You shaped the behavior and made his positive moment real. Congrats on creating a positive cycle for Max. You may need to repeat that dozens of times during the school year until he stays on task and with the class. My question to you: Will it be dozens of soul-grinding corrections for him, or does it feel organic and positive for Max as he gradually comes to his own conclusion that he needs to keep his body with the class? Does he feel like a mess-up or does he feel cared about? Does he feel as though his every decision is wrong or like a boy who can make positive decisions? If Max does not intuitively change his behavior with this type of indirect prompting, shift to social coaching (chapter 4).

Examples of TPR for Social Behaviors

- Nice looking at what your friend is playing!

- You're coming closer to her play area!

- Great job asking for a turn to play!

- You're taking turns!

- I see you two are disagreeing … Wow, you worked it out!

- What a great conversation-starter question!

- You are being so curious about your brother's class play!

- Nice follow-up question!

- Awesome job flowing with the changing conversation topic!

- You adjusted your behavior to keep her happy!

- You used your words!

- You're so flexible!

- What a wonderful compromise!

Examples of TPR for Self-Regulation/Cooperation

- Great listening!

- Thanks for thinking about me with your eyes!

- I see Suzy, Fred, Thomas, and Lila being great listeners! I'm looking for other listeners.

- Nice cooperation.

- You listened the *first time*!

- I see Elle stopping her drawing right on time!

- You are showing the group you are ready to move on to the next activity!

- Nice transition!

- Way to stop doing _____ in order to _____!

- I see Harry getting ready to _____!

- Way to stay calm and quiet!

- Awesome relaxation breathing!

- Wow, you handled that beautifully!

- I appreciate how hard you are trying!

- You calmed down. I bet that was hard!

- You didn't want to do it, but you did!

- What a great decision!

- Way to control your body!

- You scanned yourself and slowed down your engine!

- Great control over your mouth/body!

Examples of TPR for Group Work

- Nice listening to your friend's idea!

- Good suggestion. Nice job giving ideas!

- Great request for that marker. Nice asking!

- Fantastic patience!

- Way to wait for the scissors—that was hard!

- Great job seeing that your friend was working there—you didn't mess up his area!

- Nice flexibility. Way to be Bendy!

- You changed your mind!

- You kept him happy!

- Way to consider her feelings!

- Nice adjustment to keep the group working well!

Now you know the basics of interrupting negative cycles and creating positive ones. You can start practicing this skill immediately, even without all the additional social-coping skills training strategies that will follow. Good luck and enjoy. Catch and positively reflect any and every positive behavior your child performs—even ones that you already expect her to do. Why? Because you meet your child at her current level of performance ability. You validate her current abilities and successes on this lily pad.

"Do Rules": State and Publish Your Expectations as Skill-Based Positive Replacement Behaviors

By now, you are practicing the default setting of social coaching, TPR. Next, you can begin to layer in expectations for new positive behaviors. This is a form of goal setting. For younger children you can assign the skills/behaviors; in middle school and above it is most beneficial to collaboratively brainstorm for the next skill/behavior on which to focus.

For many children with SECCs, receptive auditory processing (understanding oral communication from others) can be a weaker cognitive skill. Also, children with memory retrieval issues or executive functioning challenges have trouble retaining rules and expectations. It's as if verbal rules or instructions float away into the air and the child "forgets" them. Visual spatial concepts such as rules, schedules, calendars, and time are abstract and hard to mentally organize and retain.

However, when information is concrete, permanent, visible, or tangible, something great happens. Functioning improves for the child with SECCs. Visual calendars or clocks are simple tools that decrease anxiety and increase cooperation and understanding for this population. Checklists for homework or bedtime hygiene routines help make children successful and more independent at these tasks. In my experience, writing and drawing social-coping lessons on flip chart paper makes the concepts concrete, understandable, memorable, and permanent; we can refer to them later, as well. In my programs, any time we want to increase practice of a skill or set a new clear rule of conduct, we **W.P.P.** it. **Write, Publish, and Post** your expectations and rules to help your child make better choices, cooperate, and practice positive replacement behaviors.

Write publish and post your top "Do Rules". "Increase-Behaviors" are those you want your child to start doing—or do more frequently. Think about your child in your home or classroom. What are the top three-to-five specific behaviors that would help the child succeed socially? How about academically? What behaviors would most help your family or classroom feel/function better? Jot them down brainstorming style. For your first attempt, try for at least three. If you wind up with more than five, you should read them over again and assess whether any of them can easily be combined. Preschoolers can't handle more than three Increase-Behaviors at a time. As not to overwhelm the older child, edit hard and delete anything over five rules. It's a long life, and you can always get to more advanced skills/behaviors later. You may have to prioritize by asking yourself, "what three-to-five things will make the biggest difference in her life/our family/ the classroom right now?"

There is a success-oriented way to write Do Rules. Be brief. Don't use wordy phrases or sentences. Use as few words as possible and say exactly what you want to see or hear your child do.

Remember that we are trying to create positive cycles. You're asking your child to start performing new social-coping skills behaviors on top of the baseline strengths for which you are giving TPR. Therefore, Do Rules should not start with the words "Stop" or "No." Rules like "No hitting" or "Stop interrupting" are in the negative formulation, and should be saved for "Decrease-Behaviors." While the spirit of the request is fine, asking a child with SECCs to simply stop an unhelpful behavior will likely lead to frustration on everyone's part. Negative cycles. You didn't provide the child with a positive behavior to replace the stopped behavior, so your child will slide right back into old habits. You'll be frustrated and probably correct her, "Why can't you stop interrupting?"

Instead, Do Rules are designed to give your child a positive thing to do *in place of* the ineffective alternative. Do Rules can include social-coping skills your child learned in therapy. Therefore, when you write a Do Rule, to be sure that it is a positive replacement behavior. While you are getting started, imagine parenthetically the word "Do" at the beginning of each statement (even though it makes for a clunky sentence) Consider these:

- [Do] Follow directions the first time you are asked

- [Do] Use your calming strategies from Mr. Mike's office

- [Do] Use kind words and voices

- [Do] Share with your siblings

- [Do] Try to be "Bendy" (flexible) and change your mind on purpose, when it will be helpful

Avoid generalities at all costs. "Be good" or "Show respect" are too general and subjective, and leave a lot of room for interpretation, which is kryptonite for the child with SECCs. Instead, you need to create expectations that describe exactly what you want to see or hear out of your child. If you state the precise behavior, the child can then follow through.

By Writing, Publishing, and Posting the Do Rules your child now has specific objectives to strive for. Your job is to strongly reinforce your child's practice of the Do Rules with TPR.

Remember the baseline of positivity you established with TPR? Now, when a Do Rule is performed, be sure to give extra-enthusiastic TPR and a hug or high five when your child accomplishes one of these key behaviors. You need to validate that the Do Rule behavior was performed and emphasize that it is the precise success you would like to see repeated. For example, "What a lovely compliment for your sister, Emily."

The Do Rule list is flexible and not set in stone. When your child consistently performs one of the rules you can have a "graduation ceremony" in which your child strikes it off the list. You can then suggest the addition of a new Do Rule (perhaps one that you struck from the list earlier but wanted to get back to). Say, "This rule of using kind words and voices is getting so easy for you. I still expect you to do it, but now let's write a new rule to put in its place." This is how you can gradually, in step-by-step fashion, increase your child's social development. Keep crossing off mastered Do Rules and raising the bar. You will baby-step your child to success.

To maintain a positive cycle, aim for *ten* TPRs for every *one* direct correction. If that seems daunting, remember, you can't fail at this. Just do your best out of your intense desire for your child to learn the skills he needs. If you fall short of the 10:1 ratio and instead "only" deliver 7:1 or 5:1 ratios, don't worry, that's pretty darn good.

You can create the culture of positivity in a group setting, too. In a group, family, or classroom setting, sprinkle TPR around liberally. As soon as you deliver it to one child, have your eyes scan the other children for praiseworthy moments.

The Do Rule List and TPR can be incorporated neatly into the sloppy, relationship-based reward system that will be discussed later in this book.

Selective Attention: Targeted Ignoring

By now, I hope you understand the importance of creating positive cycles in order to elicit positive replacement skills and behaviors. The very first skill we named was **positive attention**. The type of behaviors to which you attend determines whether you build your child up or contribute to a frustrated status quo.

Remember the ten-to-one TPR to correction ratio? How do we limit behavior correction to one in ten opportunities? In social-coping skills development, the formula I espouse is to reinforce and reward liberally but correct and coach selectively.

Reflect most positive behaviors, but only coach or correct your child on up to three select challenging behaviors that you choose thoughtfully and proactively. Prepare your mind to coach only high-priority social/behavioral challenges so your child doesn't think she is always wrong or always in trouble. Not only do I give you permission to overlook minor miscues that aren't that important, I want you to intentionally do so. Decide not to comment on behaviors that are not things you are working on with your child. We call this **Targeted Ignoring**.

Targeted Ignoring is beneficial for behavioral training. Ignoring "minor" negative behaviors (and most unwanted behaviors are just that) creates an attention vacuum for them. Negative behaviors are not fed (reinforced) by your attention. They are not validated (made real), and most will fade away when starved of attention. Once you set up this culture of positive attention and targeted ignoring, you will find that most kids choose more effective behaviors simply because they get more out of them. They get attention, social contact, and academic success. In my experience, most minor nuisance behaviors organically fall by the wayside when children focus on producing more and more positive behaviors.

Let's further refine the thought process for targeted ignoring. What makes a behavior "minor?" It's all relative. It depends on the child and the situation. There are two criteria that you can use for spot assessment of what to do. You must think about the behavior's **impact** and **functionality**.

First, assess whether your child's behavior impacted anyone. "Does this behavior directly disturb someone's peace?" "Did it hurt their feelings or harm their process?" You can usually tell if someone was impacted. Nonverbal social cues are your guide. Does the peer make a pained or angry face or does her expression remain the same? Does she turn her back or push your child away to create distance, or does she stay calm and engaged with your child? Does her voice turn stern and frustrated or not? These are all social cues your child may miss.

Remember, the goal is your child's development of social awareness and skill. Your best shot at teaching perspective-taking is if the affected person provides an obvious reaction for you to point out. Then you might jump in with cause-and-effect social coaching. Use the person's reaction to develop the ability to take others' perspective. "Take a look at her face right now … does she look happy or upset? She didn't like it when you _____. What can you do to help her feel better right now?" If the peer didn't show an appreciable reaction, then you should decide to let it go. Without a concrete reaction to use, your social coaching is toothless.

For example, your child sees a peer wearing a Pokemon t-shirt. She is overly honest with her opinion. "Pokemon is for babies," she says. Most adults would cringe because that comment sounds unkind. Your former self may have leapt to correct that remark. However, the unfazed peer barely registered it and continued talking to your child. What do you do? Decide to let it go. Save the correction for a time when the peer *does* negatively react to your child.

Some caregivers challenge me on this issue, "But that was mean. She shouldn't get away with it." My answer is that there are so many opportunities to correct your child, that you could correct all day long, but we know that overcorrection impedes social-coping skills development. If the peer doesn't react you have no concrete evidence, or social cues, to point out. To teach perspective-taking it is immensely helpful to be able to show your child the peer's facial expression or tone of voice. Your correction will have more impact if you can use a peer's negative reaction as an example of a social cue for your child to read and interpret. Without it, your intervention comes off as just another bossy correction by another bossy adult. When in doubt, Targeted Ignore. You'll know clearly if a behavior impacted someone else.

Second, assess each behavior's impact on the functioning of your child and of the group. Does the behavior allow tasks and activities to function or prevent things from functioning? Does it block, disrupt, or interrupt the process of the home, school, or extracurricular activity? If, due to the behavior, a caregiver can't safely drive, or a teacher can't complete instructions due to interruptions, then you must intervene. If you can still complete your task despite slightly bothersome but not disruptive behavior, Targeted Ignore. Let it go. Can you differentiate the big deal that needs immediate redirection from the smaller deal that needs ignoring?

Ask yourself, "Does this behavior prevent me from doing what I have to do?" "Does this behavior make it impossible to get through this group/classroom/family task?" "Does this behavior make my child unable to complete her own task/chore/work?" You are literally weighing in real time whether the behavior allows things to work for the child and the larger group—or not. These are questions of function. "Does this action prevent my child from functioning in this setting?" "Does this behavior make the setting non-functional for others?"

A classroom example may illuminate this concept. Donna is a fourth-grade child with excessive energy and movement. It is hard for her to sit still in class. Mrs. Flannigan, Donna's understanding teacher, permits her to take a lap around the classroom anytime she gets restless. If Donna takes her movement break without distracting peers, Mrs. Flannigan uses targeted ignoring. If she stops at a peer's desk to chat, it distracts the peer, so the teacher chooses to redirect. Finger fidget manipulative objects are often used to help children with SECCs concentrate in class. When fidgets are effective, they provide a healthy release of movement energy and the child focuses on the lesson. Targeted Ignoring. When the fidget becomes a toy and the child's and classmates' eyes and attention are solely on the fidget, the teacher must intervene.

To me, undesirable behaviors that still allow for functioning are stylistic nuisances but are secondary to disruptive behaviors. Sure, your child's behavior could be less nudgy. Maybe it could be more efficient, but it doesn't really harm anything. In basketball terms, "No harm, no foul." Let it go. That's Targeted Ignoring, a.k.a. selective intervention.

Red Phase behavior that is out of control always rises to priority level. Meltdowns, elopements, or other loss of control cannot be ignored and must be supported (with guidance from Emotional GPS). If your child struggles with self-regulation, that becomes the highest priority in treatment and goal setting. "If you're freaking out, you can't do social." Self-regulation is a higher priority than social skills, because for dysregulated children, the most emotional energy is focused internally on staying calm. There isn't enough mental bandwidth to devote to great socialization. Your child can't really focus outside of herself and on others very well. Therefore, it is compassionate and strategic to first focus on the regulation piece. Several early Do Rules and support should center around self-regulation, which includes frustration and temper prevention strategies and a safety plan for the Red Phase. Once your child improves her emotion regulation, then you can target social skills.

Warning. The suggestion to intentionally ignore unhelpful/unwanted behaviors may be emotionally triggering for you. You read here that you are supposed to let certain things go. However, you challenge this notion. "What if the behavior never gets better—or even gets worse while we are ignoring it?" "I'm not doing my job as caregiver if I don't help her with this." I empathize deeply and profoundly and have felt the same way at various times as a therapist and as a parent. I wished so many times that I could work on everything all at once. This is incredibly hard on caregivers who intensely wish their children could be OK … *yesterday*. Same thing goes for the child who has multiple complex disruptive behavior challenges. However, there are huge benefits if you can prioritize behaviors to work on and let most "minor" things go until later.

Consider the example of the child who has not yet learned the social skill of reciprocal conversation. Meet Sam, who seems to "talk at" his peers, and tells them everything he knows about reptiles. Sam doesn't ask Mark about Mark's interests. You know the big picture and know that over time, Mark might get bored of hearing about reptiles. You worry that Mark will start ignoring Sam or end the friendship. Reciprocal conversation is an important social skill, for sure.

This is something to be aware of, and I share your concern about the *conversation skills*. It is absolutely a skill that will benefit Sam personally, educationally, and professionally. However, Sam also currently *refuses to do homework* (non-functional), is *disrespectful to teachers and parents* (disruptive to group functioning), and occasionally visits the Red Phase in the form of *rage attacks* (non-functional). If you attempt to address everything at once, Sam will be overwhelmed, confused, and unable to even consider the conversation skills. Addressing too many things may be contributing to Sam's anger. We need to prioritize.

Let's create a hierarchy of the behaviors to focus on, in terms of the behaviors that have the most immediate negative impact to the least. Take a minute to think or write the four behaviors in *italics* in the previous paragraph. Put them into an order of priority. Which would you address first, second, third, and fourth?

Here are my priorities:

1. Decrease frequency and intensity of rage attacks; decrease recovery time

2. Explore and problem-solve the homework issue

3. Improve respectful communication with adults

4. Develop age-appropriate reciprocal conversation skills

Of course, these are all arguable, and in your home or classroom, you may place these behaviors in a slightly different order. My thought process is as follows: I made rage attacks and homework numbers one and two because they have to do with functionality. When Sam is in the Red Phase, he can't do anything productive, and in fact, he can be physically and emotionally hurtful. Sam's refusal to do homework is non-functional. He is not doing his developmental tasks. Respectful communication with adults and conversation skills are lower priorities in my mind, because they are more about quality of life and interaction style. We can get to them next as soon as things are more under control.

With selective intervention and targeted ignoring you intentionally decide, "I am not going to correct X, Y, and Z, for now. I can always get to them later. It's a long life. For now, I will focus on A, B, and C."

Exercise: Behavior Priority List

Now, apply this prioritization to your own child with SECCs. Grab a pen and a piece of paper. Find a quiet and private place to sit where you will be able to take your time and think clearly. On the left side of the paper, write a list of all your child's behaviors that concern you. Don't worry about placing them in any particular order. Brainstorm to make your list exhaustive, and then rate each behavior on a scale of 0-10. Zero indicates a minor behavior that has no impact on another person and is functional (nothing is disrupted). A rating of ten designates a behavior that greatly impacts others or is disruptive or destructive to the present task, activity, or the group. Take a few minutes to rate the behaviors.

Next, read over your list and review each behavior and its rating. Do any ratings need to be adjusted? After you feel that each behavior is accurately rated, rewrite the list of behaviors in descending value. Start with the highest-rated behavior(s) and work your way down to the lower ones. You have just created a behavior priority list. You can use this to create your list of no more than five Do Rules (three for preschoolers). Notice, the most intense, disruptive, and impactful behaviors are on top. It's no big deal if you have a few behaviors that are rated the same.

You now have a roadmap to guide your child's social-coping skills training. Give TPR for all the behaviors but provide extra enthusiasm for current ones you are prioritizing. For behavioral correction or social coaching, decide to ignore any lower priority behaviors and don't comment on them until it is their time. Once your child demonstrates consistent improvement in one of the top behaviors, cross it off the list and begin to target the next one down.

Frame and Reframe: Celebrate baby steps. We all have our own personal dreams for our children. We root with all our heart for our child to succeed. We practically need it! It's interesting that long-term goals for your child sometimes turn into expectations that they *should* be a certain way.

Strong expectations and needs come from a place of passion, which is a double-edged sword. Your passion may be what drives you to advocate courageously for your child's needs. That passion fuels your endurance to keep pursuing the next therapy and the next support to help her succeed. However, cognitive behavioral therapy tells us that passionate expectations also may set you up for disappointment. Be cognizant of your expectations, as well as personal hopes and needs.

Passion and expectations are the lifeblood of sports. Fans root, root, root for the home team, and if they don't win, fans are disappointed, some to the point of devastation. Perhaps they even "boo" their displeasure if they feel their beloved team underperformed their expectations. Caregivers are at risk of accidentally communicating disappointment toward the child with SECCs based on our passion and our hopes.

Countless parents have tearfully confided in me that they fear that their child "won't be okay" or "won't make it as an adult." Because of the intensity of their love for their child, when they see slow progress in the present, they panic. Anxiety of an unknown future creates internal pressure for the loving caregiver. "She needs to get this skill *now*." "How will she be ready to go off to college or hold a job?"

Therefore, the caregiver as social-coping skills trainer must monitor internal reactions to a child's repeated miscues or major mishaps. Emotional responses such as disappointment or anxiety/panic activate the impulse to act. They trigger the instantaneous urge to do something to decrease your internal tension. If your child makes a social miscue or disrupts, your impulse may be to catch and correct, yell and vent, or cry and withdraw. It can be hard to hide these and other reactions, and you may accidentally leak impatience or frustration over something your child with SECCs can't control. Even children who miss social cues can be sensitive to your mood and feelings. Unintentional expressions of disappointment or impulsive correction can so easily reactivate the negative cycle.

Be aware of your expectations and your impulses. Therapists are taught to observe their internal states and deactivate their automatic knee jerk reactions. Get curious about your internal sensations. "Why did I just get such a strong emotional reaction to that mess-up?" Please note that this section in no way asks you to divorce yourself from emotion and become an unfeeling robot. Lord knows, you are justified to have so much love, care, passion, and concern for your struggling child. However, I think we'll agree that it is a worthy objective to decrease caregivers' impulsive reactions that slow or regress social-coping development.

There is a way to counteract the tendency to become overwhelmed by fear of the far-flung future or expectations: Get in the now. Adopt a **Baby-Step Philosophy** in the present. Let's get our expectations in sync. Out of thousands of parent and teacher interactions, along with my observations of clients and campers, I have developed a set of real-life, realistic expectations of children with SECCs:

- Children with SECCs are strongly influenced by their brain wiring, which is not the same as neurotypical folks. They process, behave, and regulate differently than the average kid.

- Cognitive gaps in social awareness, flexibility, problem solving, self-regulation, etc. are the cause of social and behavioral mistakes. They are (usually) not personal and never come at a "convenient" time for caregivers.

- Your child can't help it. If she could behave better in that moment, she would.

- Your child is trying to function as best as she can at any given time. It's hard. She is more prone to influence by wiring, hunger, tiredness, and environmental factors than the average person.

- Many people describe children with SECCs as "consistently inconsistent" and "predictably unpredictable" because they seemingly have better-functioning days and worse-functioning days, or parts of days, for no apparent reason. We need to celebrate the successful times and compassionately coach through the rough ones.

- Social skills training and development is gradual and not a straight path. We need to accept the reality that it is "two steps forward, one step back."

- Developing textbook social-coping skills is the goal, but kids don't snap their fingers and instantly display perfect and sophisticated skills. First a child shows 25% mastery, then 35%, then 50%, then 70% mastery on the way to 90% success. We need to expect gradual progress with possible plateaus along the path toward the desired goal.

- Nobody is perfect.

I find these truths liberating, because they allow us to let go of false expectations. Embrace the imperfect reality and trust the process. Let's adopt an appreciation for *approximation* of a goal. We'll begin by examining a sample scenario: Your child used to be anxious and avoided birthday parties, but finally feels comfortable going to a birthday party at the age of 9. Don't say, "Yeah, but she missed out on all the birthday parties in first and second grade." Instead, praise and celebrate the 9-year-old's success.

Let's extend the birthday party scenario. Notice your hope and expectations when your child attends her first party: You hoped she could join in and enjoy the party activities. You dreamed of the day she could be in the peer group, and now, this birthday party is her chance. Your heart aches for your child as you wish for her to be comfortable with and enjoy these true childhood moments. Considering these hopes, how do you feel if your child attaches to your hip and remains on the periphery of the party? What if she nervously watches the fun activities but doesn't join the other kids? You might problem-solve on the car ride home to prepare her for the next birthday party. That is one way to frame the experience, but at what cost? Your child may feel as though she can't do anything right. "Can't I get credit for going to the party, which was really hard for me?"

Stay in the now. Let's celebrate the baby step and reframe the experience as a positive. It's a (huge) baby step that she got there. Targeted Positive Reflection would be, "I am so proud that you were brave and ready to go to the party." "It was a great idea to stand on the side and observe today. Now you know what to expect." "I wonder how you will join in at the next party?"

Reframe the behavior as one successful baby step out of many on a larger path of growth. Doing so embeds a subconscious message of acceptance in your child's mind. "This behavior is good enough today." "You can do this." The baby step approach keeps you and your child in the present. Essentially, what you are telling her is you accept her abilities today with a hopeful eye on tomorrow.

Use baby steps to set realistic social skills/behavior goals with your child. If it used to require five reminders for her to brush her teeth, then make a baby-step goal of three reminders, and then give TPR for that success. Let her enjoy the new level of success for a few weeks, and the three-reminder pattern will become the new baseline. (Remember the lily pad analogy?) After three weeks of TPR, say, "Boy, it's getting too easy for you to do that … see if you can do it with me only reminding you once or twice." Think of each baby step the child makes toward the full goal as a success in and of itself. Give TPR.

Strengthen Positive Cycles with a Sloppy, Relationship-Based, Carnival-Style Reward System

Sometimes, Targeted Positive Reflection does not provide as much clarity or strength of reinforcement as we may want. Difficulty with social communication skills or more profound processing/Autism challenges can make it hard for positive social feedback to trigger the happy (reinforcing) brain chemicals of dopamine, oxytocin, and serotonin. These chemicals are usually released when the brain perceives success, relief, happiness, pride, closeness, and other "positive feelings" (notice the value judgement; feelings are neither positive nor negative). Pleasure chemicals bathe the brain and body when social experiences and interactions are perceived as positive. There are several reasons why a child with SECCs might not experience the neurological wave of pleasure that carry the message, "That's great, do that again to get more good feelings:"

- Weakness in receptive language ability and slow processing speed may make it difficult to immediately comprehend verbally communicated praise.

- Some kids with SECCs are more likely to misread or simply not notice subtle positive non-verbal and tone-of-voice cues, so they don't receive the message (subtle non-verbal gestures, tone of voice) that would trigger the rewarding chemicals. They need concrete and explicit positive reinforcement in order to correctly read it as positive.

- Stimulus-hungry, poorly regulated or emotionally reactive children tend to obey internal tensions and feelings. They focus mostly on relief of their own internal tensions. Some children with SECCs pursue internal pleasure and avoid discomfort at all costs. This means that they are guided less by external positives (TPR) and walk to the beat of their own drum.

- The child who presents with prolonged egocentrism wants to get her way to the exclusion of others' needs. Hoping to receive preferred pleasures and avoid tension and discomfort, this child might not easily do what you ask if she can't see what's in it for her.

- Years of habitual reliance on old, ineffectual social-coping patterns may have solidified them. Changing years-long patterns and habits is difficult for anyone, let alone for kids who are neurologically rigid-minded. We can't just *ask* someone to stop doing something that they have been doing for six, ten, or fifteen years and expect that the old habits will change on demand.

Hypothetically, let's say you faithfully follow the method of creating positive cycles through TPR but don't see much—or any—progress. You don't see the baby-step improvements you'd hoped for in cooperation and in social skills. Perhaps your Do Rules are not being followed. Your child continues to make the same old social faux pas.

This is not completely unexpected and sometimes happens in the therapy process with clients. Caregivers who have been grappling with these issues for a long time shouldn't interpret it as your failure or your child's inability to learn this stuff. It doesn't mean your therapist is incompetent (says the therapist.). Don't panic. Take it as a signal that your child might need a stronger and more overt (concrete) reinforcement structure.

External and concrete rewards (along with methodically applied consequences) are the tools to strengthen social-coping skills development. At this point I want to power you up with a unique, positive behavior reward system. You will strengthen and concretize the positive cycle so that your child sees it and feels it. External positive reinforcement can make many children more motivated to try. This reward system is a training strategy to stack on top of your existing TPR skills.

Reward System Overview

Through research, experimentation, failures, and successes, I developed a positive behavior reinforcement system. It is founded on behavioral principles, though funneled through a child-centered filter and observed through a relationship-based lens.

It is not as formal as Applied Behavioral Analysis, and it is not boring and futile, like sticker charts. Sticker charts usually review a span of time such as a morning/afterschool time, a school day, or a class period to evaluate whether a child performed a prescribed behavior. When you review an earlier time period you are just as likely to notice a child's misbehavior or non-behavior. You've effectively caught your child messing up. Then, when she *doesn't* earn the sticker or star you negatively reinforce your child for her shortcoming. What if your child spent 99% of the time successfully but made one misstep? That one misstep precludes your child from gaining her sticker. Is this the positive cycle your child needs? Does this provide feedback in real time like TPR? It does not. Countless parents have complained about sticker charts and told me that they would inevitably forget to use them anyway. Please scrap the sticker chart if it is not working for your child. I don't want to advocate too strongly against sticker charts; they can help sometimes. If it happens to work for your child and you, congratulations. Keep it up. (It's all about function.)

Remember, in real-time social interactions, children with SECCs have a hard time discerning whether their behavior was effective or not. They are caught up in the interaction, may lack self-awareness, or be impulsive. Providing a belated sticker as a form of reinforcement doesn't help your child develop self-awareness in real time. Also, those types of reward systems are neither nimble nor flexible. If you want to change them, you need to wait until a convenient time to delete or re-write the chart. In my clinical experience and opinion, the reward/feedback system should be nimble, provide instantaneous feedback, and tell the child exactly which behavior was positive. Real-time feedback helps the child identify the behaviors that are better to repeat—or stop.

The second problem with sticker charts is forgetting. By the time a child learns that she did not earn a sticker or star, the offending behavior may have happened minutes or even hours earlier. The child may forget (or deny) that it happened. She may become defensive and argue with the caregiver. If social and behavioral learning is the goal, it seems diminished by the retrospective evaluation.

Worse still for the child with SECCs, the sticker chart doesn't allow credit for partial performance (baby step) of a skill. How do you baby step toward a desired goal that requires positive reinforcement when sticker charts play "gotcha" with kids? You wind up "catching" non-performance of skills, which results in a negative communication, such as, "So sorry … you screwed up, and, no, you don't get that sticker." The child feels, "You don't like me and never give me credit. I was so good the rest of the period. Don't you care about all the good things I do?" Does this make the child feel safe and closer to the caregiver? Unlikely.

Hundreds of parents and teachers have attested to me that our unique brand of reinforcement is doable for adults and meaningful for their children. It's a game-changer. Because it occurs in the flow of your day and is attached to your actual interactions and relationship with your child, it becomes a part of life. One outcome study into the efficacy of the Camp Pegasus program suggests that children decrease unexpected behaviors and increase expected (pro-social) behaviors.[1] A second outcome study indicated that participants also improve executive functioning skills in the same eight-week summer program.[2] While the studies didn't research the efficacy of this reward system in isolation, it is one key ingredient in the total social training approach in this successful program.

---

[1] Brodoff, R. (2017) Examining the effectiveness of a summer camp for improving the social skills and self-regulation behaviors in children with Autism Spectrum Disorder (Doctoral Dissertation). Retrieved from Proquest (Accession No. 10286756).

[2] Terrell, K. (2019) Evaluating a social skills intervention's impact on executive functioning among children with Autism spectrum disorder and social skills deficits (Doctoral Dissertation). Retrieved from Proquest (Publication No. 13896410).

The sloppy, relationship-based, carnival-style reward system I propose here is a token system that piggybacks neatly on top of the TPR you have been practicing. Children continue to receive TPR for positive behaviors that contribute to socialization, family life, and classroom functioning. Simultaneous to giving the Targeted Positive Reflection, the caregiver gives one or more tokens. Thus, children receive, in real time, positive feedback for desired behaviors along with a concrete token magnifying that moment. Children know that the token leads toward a desired prize or preferred activity (more details later).

By pursuing a prize, the child finds **external motivation** that often overrides her internal motivation and habits. Internal motivation could be any number of things: a rigid preference for sameness, avoidance of anxiety-provoking situations, pursuit of preferred activities, or simply wanting to engage in familiar behaviors rather than trying new ones. When we provide external motivation in the form of tokens or rewards, we see children behave more cooperatively and consider breaking old patterns. The child seems to find just a little more tolerance for problem-solving and attention span for less-preferred activities. Parents and teachers report that children seem far more willing to try new experiences and social-coping skills due to the external motivation from the reward system.

A secondary benefit of the reward system is *enhanced self-awareness*. Children seem to think just a little bit harder about each decision and behavior. We notice that they keep in mind the Emotional GPS, work harder to consider others' feelings and needs, and select more appropriate behaviors. Because of the lure of tokens toward a desired prize, the children—often for the first time—practice self-awareness and mindful decision making. Brain imaging studies have universally shown that, like muscles, parts of the brain that are exercised get stronger. Repeating new, positive social cognition and behaviors blossoms neural pathways and facilitates development of new, positive habits.

The tokens we use in our therapy groups and summer camp are colorful paperclips we call "chips." Classrooms in which I consult use marbles, popsicle sticks, or paper clips. For home reward systems, we draw "funny money" that caregivers dole out along with TPR. From now on I will call the tokens *chips* for simplicity. The action of giving chips with TPR is called *chipping*.

You can give chips to each individual child in a group or family in their own respective container. This is useful if you want to differentiate the behaviors/skills for which each child will be rewarded. Each child can watch her chip amount increase with anticipation of the eventual prize.

You can also adapt the program for use with a whole group, classroom, or family system. Make it a team effort reinforcing and motivating a group-wide culture of positive social-coping by collecting all the kids' chips in one large container. Collective chipping makes social-coping improvement a group project. "We're all in this together." You can help children discover that human beings are interdependent, "You're all counting on each other to follow our group Do Rule list so you can earn the group prize."

Speaking plainly, this reward system strives to "catch kids being good," meaning you can give TPR for any positive behavior. "Thank you for helping Johnny find his lost highlighter!" "I like how you held the door for us!" This TPR and chipping begins with credit for the easy positives that the child or group already perform. It's as if your actions say to the child, "See, I *do* recognize the things you do." Just give one or two chips for a commonplace positive.

Reflecting and rewarding the small things creates the desired atmosphere of positivity and recognizes the child for contributing goodness to her world. Recognition is an investment in the child's emotional fund of resilience. By filling her bank account with small victories, the child is more amenable to giving effort toward your more challenging Do Rules.

The child who often uses control as a coping mechanism (in extreme cases diagnosed with Oppositional Defiant Disorder) habitually reacts to demands and expectations with resistance and power struggles. Caregivers' requests and behavioral goals are often perceived as unwelcome external threats and things to oppose. We notice that oppositional clients and campers are disarmed by this "passive" reward system used in conjunction with Jeopardy Coaching.

Think of it this way: When you demand or correct, you state a position or expectation. Like an explorer planting a flag claiming your ground, directive or declarative statements tend to imply that you own the land called *control*. Your child, who has an overdeveloped need to feel in control, feels threatened or anxious by your flag, so she resists you. She pushes back against your firmness. The brilliance of the Art of Friendship approach is that the oppositional child finds fewer things to oppose. You start with TPR. Then you add rewards. And you use Jeopardy Coaching. Your child gains the benefits of social training and coaching, but you decrease opportunity for power struggles.

I want to proactively problem solve a potential bug in the system. Every so often, we come across the child who, at first, defiantly declares, "I don't care about prizes. This reward system is stupid!" I've been there. This is clinical resistance, which is normal and expected. Try not to get discouraged or take it personally. This is a prime example of the powerful and controlling child trying to shut down the system before it gets started. Even ultra-positive change is still change, which may provoke anxiety and resistance.

Don't be controlled and don't back down from our positivity plan. My answer is, "Well, this is just what we are doing *for a while*, and we will be noticing and commenting on the positive things you do. Even if you don't want the chips, we will put them in a container for you in case you want to count them later and get prizes. We'll see how you feel about it later. Now, let's talk about the prizes you can earn; what reward would you like to earn?" You can also ask it this way, "What do you think you might be willing to work toward?" How many kids will turn down a prize? Then, you plow ahead with your unrelenting TPR and chips. When the child earns her first prize, let's see if she still rejects it. (She won't.) Now, you've got her hooked. You win. She wins. Behavioral shaping is on the way.

How to Implement the Reward System

Give your child as much control in the rewards system design process as possible to help with her buy-in.

- Design tokens, or "bucks" or "**chips**," a.k.a. funny money. You are going to carry tokens with you wherever you go all day long. In large group situations like school, camp, or social skills groups, use small and inexpensive items you can get in bulk, like the paper clips we use in my program.

- To personalize tokens for a child or a family, have your child design round or rectangular "funny money" on a piece of paper. Come up with a fun name for them like "Mike Money," "Dori Dollars," or "Brandon Bucks." They could also be called "Fun Bucks" or anything your child wants. Have fun with it. Photocopy the bucks so that when you cut them out, there will be ninety to 100 tokens per child. You can have fun with it by printing in color or copying on colorful copy paper selected by your child. If you don't have access to a copier, no worries; simply draw out enough bucks freehand. Every morning simply grab a stack of bucks and shove them in your bag or pocket. You are armed and ready to power up your child's behavioral learning.

- Give sloppily. "No rules ... just right." Give as much or as little as you want. You are already practicing TPR, and now attach bucks to the enthusiasm of your reflection. Oh no, this is not an anal-retentive sticker chart. In fact, randomizing your chipping *strengthens* the child's performance, so it is even okay if you are not perfect and happen to miss an opportunity to give. Tell your child, "I'm sorry, I want to catch as many of these great things as possible, but I'm only human and I missed one. I'll try to catch the next one." You are modeling that it is okay to be imperfect, which itself has value.

I suggest following these loose chipping guidelines:

Begin with a baseline of giving TPR plus one chip for routine and expected positive behaviors. Some caregivers say, "I'm not rewarding my kid for doing things I know she already can do." I second this notion in principle. However, when you begin this reward system, you want to generate buy-in. You want her to invest in the process. If you begin by rewarding only new and challenging social-coping skills, your child might not get many chips or prizes. She may feel discouraged when she inconsistently performs the desired Do Rule list of skills. The child who tends toward resistance or oppositional behavior may fight it. Your positivity might not outweigh the negative feedback loop I discussed earlier.

You and your child will find more success by beginning the reward program with current competencies. It's called "meeting your child where she is." When you begin by giving TPR and tokens for the many baseline behaviors she is *already* good at, she will feel recognized and appreciated. She will sense that she can be successful. She will feel as though you have shifted from an adversary to an ally. You may see your child's spirits lift, which is a sign that her brain is showering her with the pleasure chemicals that reinforce and encourage the repetition of the behaviors you desire.

By starting with easy successes, you create baseline expectations. Even on a "bad day," at least your child can still do these simple positive behaviors (e.g. manners, helping, following basic directions). Once your child experiences a few days of recognition and reward for baseline pro-social behaviors, you can add Do Rules, raise expectations, and notice the more advanced or desired behaviors.

Expand the reward system to greater impact when your child overcomes a huge challenge or tries a new coping skill for the first time. Let your excitement show when your child performs a new or desired social-coping behavior by altering your volume and tone of voice. Exclaim, "You did it. That's the first time you stayed calm when you were frustrated." Feel free to offer a "sloppy handful" of bonus chips (and fork over a ridiculous pile of chips). Match the chip amount and your tone of voice to your enthusiasm for the behavior. In this way, it moves beyond the "anal-retentive" and clinical-feeling sticker chart used for behavior tracking. "Sloppiness" randomizes the positive feedback, which is known to be more effective in behavioral training. It is relationship-based and an expression of your passionate cheerleading. Therefore, I call it a "sloppy, relationship-based reward system." Read on to find out why we call it "Carnival Style."

Individualize in group settings. What is the culture or values you want your group to live by? Begin with class-wide or family-wide Do Rules for all the children. Some teachers/group leaders collaborate with their children to write a classroom constitution or charter. Other times, caregivers think about family values or the school mission/vision on which to base the group-wide guidelines. These set the cultural and behavioral expectations for your setting. Give TPR plus one chip for following the rules (you will randomize it by missing a few opportunities). Following the basic rules should be doable for most of the class.

Group-wide TPR plus chips decreases police work. For the oppositional child, compliance is hard and counter-instinctive. Rewarding on-task peers may generate a positive response in the off-task child. By rewarding the cooperative kids, you ostensibly advertise that SOME kids are benefitting from choosing to be on task. This creates "FOMO" (fear of missing out) in the off-task child. When she sees and hears peers getting TPR plus chips, your child thinks "no fair." She snaps to self-awareness. Often, we observe the child self-correct when she perceives that other kids are getting things she isn't. TPRing and chipping the positive contributors to a group helps with general crowd control and the creation of a positive culture. By setting group-wide Do Rules and a chip system, you mold your overall group into a team that thinks a little harder about how they are engaging with each other and you (self-awareness).

Within this base group culture, you can then easily individualize social training for each child's needs. Make special "deals" with each child in your family or class based on her unique social-coping needs. W.P.P. (write, publish, and post) one or two personal Do Rules you want the child to practice. Provide your child with her own unique note card or paper with her personal Do Rules. For the child who is shy or reluctant to volunteer ideas you might offer, "Emily, you can get bonus chips for asking questions to start conversations." For the child who is overeager and calls out you can suggest, "Sam, you can get bonus chips by listening to the speaker, waiting your turn to talk, and not interrupting." For the child who needs to develop self-advocacy skills, "Phoebe, you will get bonus chips when I hear you using I-messages to stick up for yourself." "I will be noticing when you to do your special deal and giving you an extra-sloppy handful of chips." When children see that everyone gets individualized Do Rules, they learn that everyone has things to work on, which teaches and reinforces acceptance of neurodiversity.

Art of Friendship 'Chips' and Prize Rules for Group and Classroom Settings

Through years of trial and practice we discovered winning ways to employ this system. The following tips will help you avoid common pitfalls and get the best out of this reward system:

- Reward chips to kids when they use social and coping skills, for following Do Rules, and for using taught social-coping tools.

- Make the delivered chip amount match your TPR level of excitement about your child's behavior, tone of voice, and volume. Communicate how proud you are of that behavior. Use targeted ignoring or "Decrease-Behavior" techniques for unhelpful behaviors.

- Give out bonus chips at any time and for any reason—if your child does something especially difficult, kind, thoughtful, or helpful. Be thrilled for her: "Oh my gosh! That was incredible! You asked for a break instead of freaking out! Here's a sloppy handful of chips for you."

- Discourage the sharing or trading of chips among group members (unless you are pooling all the chips toward a classroom/family reward or party). It doesn't matter if a paper clip is large or small or blue or pink; they are all worth one point, so there is no trading of clips for color or size. (It creates distractions and arguments, trust me.)

- Do not allow children to ask for chips; they must wait for you to observe, praise, and give them. *You* must witness the positive behavior with your own eyes and ears. Requests for chips are not granted. Children shouldn't run in from another room and say, "I just gave a compliment … *chip please!*" Use firm and kind reassurance: "No, sorry, I missed that one; what you did sounds great. I hope I catch it the next time you do it (a self-fulfilling prophecy)." If a child gets upset that you did not notice and reward a positive behavior, try telling her that this proves that you are not perfect. "Because I'm not perfect, I don't expect you to be perfect either. We're all doing our best. I forgive your mess-ups and I hope you can forgive mine." Be sure to catch and reflect a positive behavior soon after.

Warning! Watch the urge to bribe an oppositional child with the reward system. The definition of a bribe is to coerce a person of superior power to do something. In contrast to a bribe, a reward is a donation of value in exchange for a behavior of value. Children who constantly refuse directions hyper-control the one thing they can: themselves. They grasp at power in a world that feels overwhelming, unpredictable, and out of control. Being a caregiver for the oppositional child can be infuriating because you know that you are "supposed" to be in charge. Once a powerful control-artist defies you, you may feel out of control yourself. *I feel shame and I feel anger that this little kid has checkmated me. I hate to lose. When I get in this same position, I feel desperate to regain my authority.*

In that situation, the child assumes control and is now dictating terms; you lose your proactive role and become more reactive. In the Sloppy, Relationship-Based, Carnival-Style Reward System, you should never make escalating bids to try to bribe/buy a child's cooperation. It unwittingly reinforces the child's maladaptive control and power grab. If a child is refusing something, don't say, "I'll give you ten bonus bucks if you _____... *No?* I'll give you twenty bonus bucks if you_____...*Still no?*... How about thirty? Please? *Ple-e-e-a-a-ase?*" Your child senses that she has all the power and she has you right where she wants you. She knows she can get her way and even hold out for greater and greater ransom in exchange for cooperation.

This is a dire pattern, because when a child has more power and control than the caregiver, she is unconsciously terrified. "If this caregiver can't control and contain me, then how can I control and contain *my* feelings and impulses?"

Who has all the power in this situation? You can see that the child has become unhealthily powerful and you are begging for cooperation. When a child refuses a task outright, your choice is to blow up the interaction in an explosive power struggle … or not. Even though your blood will boil with anger, you need to chalk it up as a loss, back off, and plan for next time. We may lose the metaphoric *battle* (the immediate episode) but we don't have to lose the *war* (the positive growth process). You can revisit the request/task later and *still* require your child to cooperate. Here is some great language to preserve your crucial role as the authority in charge, even when you strategically revoke a directive that your child refused: "Mommy has decided (or "your teachers have decided…") that you don't have to do this *right now*. Let's stop thinking about it and figure out what to do later." You can also try, "I'm not saying that you have to do this immediately, we can always come back to it later, when you're calm again."

To overcome this challenge, you can use the Iceberg Theory to explore the hidden compliance obstacle hiding beneath the surface behavior. For example, let's assume you "lost the battle" and need to let one refusal stand because it catches you off guard. During a subsequent peaceful moment, ask, "How come you would not get out of the car at the restaurant last time?" "What was hard about it?" With these questions, you should learn from these temporary defeats and collaborate with your child on a mutually acceptable plan for next time. When you find out the underlying blockage, brainstorm for ways to make that situation tolerable and successful next time. "How can we make sure our family can go inside the restaurant together next time?" Once you identify the problem and a solution, proactively write, publish, and share the plan. Lastly, you can offer a large buck reward for overcoming a challenge that had been so significant. You are back in charge. Then, "catch, reflect, and reward."

In school/social skills group settings, there are a few extra wrinkles to the reward system. Here are a few of the unique adaptations for use in group settings like schools or camps:

- With fewer options for consequences to shape behavior, we use a negative reinforcer called **The Chip Dump**.

- If a student completely ignores directions and doesn't listen, after the third prompt, she loses all chips for that activity period and starts collecting from zero all over again. This is the "Three Strikes, Chip Dump" intervention. Here's how you apply it when a child refuses to cooperate. You say dispassionately, "That's strike 1." (and give time for the child to comply) … Continued refusal makes you say calmly and firmly, "That's strike 2." (repeat the instruction and give time for the child to comply) … After the third refusal in your same objective tone you inform, "That's Strike 3. I'm sorry, but that's a chip dump." Then follow through and empty the child's cup of chips. You *must* follow through or else your child will know you are all empty threats and don't mean what you say. Empty threats magnify the oppositional child's power. Avoid the tentative, "Strike 2 … 2 and a half … 2 and three quarters … last chance … 3." In it, you communicate insecurity and avoidance of owning your role as the bearer of structure and consequences. You will unwittingly give your child unhealthy control and decrease their ownership of responsibility. Give a clear, "1 … 2 … 3 … Chip Dump."

- Make sure that the chip dump consequence is announced and published in advance of its use. *It should not be used as an impulsive expression of your anger.* It must be completely clear and anticipated so that the chip dump doesn't come as a surprise. If the child is aware of the risk of the Chip Dump, you create a clear choice: to get reinforcing chips or the consequence of losing them. This is a behavioral learning tool. If you have a child who serially avoids non-preferred tasks or defies adult directives, this is your leverage to teach decision making and maintain the therapeutic edge. When your child engages in refusal behaviors she needs to *feel* the frustration of the earned consequence. The frustration you induce with predictable consequences may motivate your child to avoid those feelings, choose effective social-coping behaviors, and even gain positive recognition plus chips. As a disclaimer, a single consequence is not a magic cure; don't fret that it doesn't work after one or two consequences. Your child may need several Chip Dumps to shape her behavior toward positive outcomes.

- In school or other group settings, physical or verbal hurting behavior or destruction of property gets an Automatic Chip Dump. Unlike the three-strike chip dump for noncompliance, this is earned instantly. It is not okay under any circumstance to hurt others physically or emotionally and my programs call those behaviors **Deal Breakers.** Label Deal Breakers clearly as a universal rule for the whole group. Say in a calm yet firm voice (and publish), "Hitting/insults/arguing with adults is not okay and it's an automatic chip dump." Then follow through and empty the child's cup of chips. For a more thorough discussion of Deal Breakers, see chapter five.

- After a chip dump, the child is immediately awarded a clean slate and can go right back to earning chips. You must not hold a grudge or act out on lingering frustration. Even if your nerves are shot, it's all about the student, and we want her to rebound from the major violation and return to positive behavioral striving.

- Students may not trade material prizes with other kids once they get them. It causes too many hurt feelings. Put them right in backpacks.

- There is no prize "layaway." Staff/teachers cannot "save" preferred prizes for students for later days. It is not fair. "You get what you get, and you don't get upset." Encourage your students not to decide in advance what prize they get, because their desired prize may be out of stock. Tell the child to browse what's in the prize box: "What do you see that you like right now?"

Carnival Style Prizes

To get children to embrace the reward system, make it fun and engaging. Like a carnival, set three levels of prizes—small, medium, and large. The number of chips required for each prize depends on the child's age and needs. To hook a novice child on the reward system, or for very young children, I recommend that you set the chip-levels low, for instance, at ten-twenty-thirty chips, respectively, for small-medium-large prizes. Your child won't have to wait very long to get her first prize, so she is speedily engaged. You can always set higher, more challenging target amounts for older children's prizes. If you started your child at lower prize thresholds in order to hook her and you find that you are giving out rewards too quickly, you can increase the points required to earn prizes. Say, "You have been getting so many prizes! I'm impressed; it's just getting too easy! Mommy and Daddy are going to challenge you. Now you get your small, medium, and large prizes at twenty-forty-sixty points." Other nice round reward amounts are twenty-five, fifty, and seventy-five points or even thirty-three, sixty-six, and ninety-nine chips. If you've tried everything else, this is an option that may turn the tide and help your child begin to try to practice the positive replacement behaviors you so desperately wish for.

Some caregivers are concerned about the use of material prizes. Above all else, rewards must align with your family/school values and be reasonable in size and expense. Examples of prizes may be plastic toys from OrientalTrading.com (or other online novelty companies), coupons for privileges like extra TV or iPad time, a homework pass or extra recess time, a class party, or bonus time with a preferred activity or person. Prizes don't have to cost much—or anything. When arranging a reward system with a single child, be sure to involve her in the selection of the three prize levels. That will guarantee that the prizes will motivate your child. Ask what she would like, but rest assured, you have ultimate veto power if the requests are too expensive, unrealistic, or conflict with your values. In a matter-of-fact tone, say, "That's a little too big. That's more like a birthday or Christmas present. What else would be a good large prize?"

Miscellaneous 'Chips' Notes

To start, make the prize threshold low to hook your child/class on the positivity and fun of the system.

Keep your child's earned tokens in a central location to which she has access. Let her count the tokens and get wrapped up in the intrigue of, "How much am I saving?" and "Which prize level am I going for this time?"

In the home program, kids cannot lose bucks. We use chip dumps only in group and social situations because adults have a narrower range of options for consequences. At home, tokens reflect good deeds already performed, and those good deeds should not disappear when kids mess up—and neither do their chips.

Thus far we established a compassionate, positive, and child-centered approach to the development of social-emotional coping skills. Children require Love and Limits in just the right measure, and in this chapter, we detailed the strategies to deliver Love. Skill-building in the form of Art of Friendship Social-Coping Skills Lessons, TPR, and the Sloppy, Relationship-Based Reward System feel great. You now have a system for eliciting cooperation and positive replacement social-coping behaviors. Now you can the shower your child with warmth, positivity, and connection, in service of her skill development.

It would be Pollyannaish, however, to expect that mere skill instruction and a reward system will magically transform your child. Children with SECCs have gaps in their social cognition, and you should expect your child to make mistakes. (After all, isn't that what childhood is for, anyway?) In the next chapter, we prepare to coach your child through the inevitable rough patches and social miscues.

CHAPTER 4

COACHING SOCIAL-COPING AND PROBLEM SOLVING

The child with SECCs has the figurative equivalent of a social-emotional learning disability. The Art of Friendship Social-Coping lessons are proactive and preventative. The Increase-Behavior reinforcement strategies stimulate their practice. However, social misunderstandings and miscues should be expected. Sometimes it's the complexities of the environment that overwhelm your child's coping repertoire, causing impulsive behaviors and miscues. Other times, he may simply misperceive social cues and select ineffective social-coping behaviors.

To preserve the positive cycle, we must coach compassionately and supportively, not through punitive or shaming responses. We already established that your child likely experiences a negative feedback loop from the world. How can we balance the need to help him grow from mistakes without feeling harshly criticized? Your child needs coaching with compassion. It is best to adopt a social coaching approach that begins with empathy. "I know this is hard for you."

Social coaching is a lot like being a coach in sports. Good coaches aren't hyper-controlling, critical, punitive, or lenient. A good coach is motivated for the constant improvement of the player(s) and the success of the team. Athletic coaches proactively game-plan for upcoming opponents. Similarly, social coaches anticipate upcoming social situations and let the child know what to expect. However, we can't plan for unexpected social moments. Social coaches make a game plan that is flexible and ready to shift to Plan B.

If the original game plan works and the team is winning, the coach doles out high fives and encouragement (like our TPR-chipping approach). On the other hand, when our team is losing or the opponent executes unexpected plays, the coach calls a time out. He huddles the team, assesses what's causing the lack of success, and suggests the necessary adjustments. We do the same thing as social coaches.

Social coaches provide a type of super-vision. You celebrate successes together and if things are going wrong for your child, you call a time-out and huddle up. You discuss the situation and help your child understand the factors that contribute to the challenge. Did he forget the game plan?

Did he execute his social skills ineffectively? Was the environment behaving unpredictably? The social coach helps your child adjust expectations, identify alternate coping strategies, or create a new social plan of action. Then, with an encouraging pat on the back, you send your child back out into the fray to do his best.

Children, like athletes, respond best to authenticity in a coach. If you provide social coaching to relieve your own anxiety, frustration, jealousy, embarrassment, anger, or sadness, then your interventions will not seem authentic to your child. He will sense that you are controlling, influencing, or placating. He will sense that it is about *you*. Here are the social coaching strategies my team has developed to make it all about the child:

Jeopardy Coaching and Redirection

In the television game show *Jeopardy,* contestants respond to knowledge challenges in the form of a question. Question form happens to be the best social coaching, in my clinical experience. Subtle changes in your language shifts a message from directive communication to facilitative communication. The difference between directives and questions is the difference between day and night. Your language choice impacts your child's social cognition, interaction, performance, and investment in social coaching.

When you instruct your child to perform a social behavior, for example, "Share that, please," *you* take responsibility for the social thought and your child does not. When you redirect your child, "Johnny, get back in your seat," *you* think about the expectation, your child does not. Functionally, adult instruction denies your child the opportunity to evaluate the social moment or a peer's needs. This is a missed learning opportunity.

More challenging still, your directive creates an internal conflict. As I mentioned earlier, the child with a high need for control may perceive a directive as an external threat to his self-control. It forces him to decide whether to comply with you. It's a limited (binary) choice of, "Do I cooperate or not?" Consider, with the command, "You need to take turns," does your child stop to consider the peer's feelings or the social context? Maybe not. He thinks, "do I want to listen to my caregiver?" It's a missed opportunity for your child to think socially. Unwittingly, your top-down directives decrease his independence and increase his dependence on you to navigate the social world.

It's absolutely crucial to give your child the responsibility of thinking socially. It is the greatest gift you can give. When you coach your child in question form, you make him practice thinking through social situations. Next, I will list sample directive statements, followed by the Jeopardy Coaching version in question form:

- "Get back in your seat."

    o "Where is your body supposed to be right now?"

- "You hurt her feelings. Tell her you're sorry."

  o "How does she feel right now? Do you want your friend to feel that way? What can you do to help your friend feel better?"

- "You didn't write down your assignment and now you will get a zero on that assignment. You need to use your assignment book."

  o "How did that work out for you? What could you do next time to remember your homework?"

- "Your friend is speaking to you. Talk to your friend."

  o "What would be a great conversation-question to ask here? What else can you learn about your friend's weekend?"

- "Calm down. I'm sending your friend home if you don't stop arguing with her."

  o "What behavior is your Road to Success/Happiness? (an Art of Friendship Social-Coping concept) What can you do to get back to fun?"

- "For the tenth time, turn off the iPad and go get ready for bed."

  o "Johnny, look at me. I need your eyes. What part of the night are we up to?" [Johnny: "Bedtime"] "What do you need to do right now if you want me read to you?"

This approach may take an extra minute, but it is an investment in your child's social development. You give your child the gift of thinking situationally and socially and converting it to productive action. As soon as you see his course correct, shift right into sloppy TPR.

A second benefit of Jeopardy Coaching is decreased battles for control and need for power struggles. Question-based coaching moves you toward a collaborative relationship. Think of all the time you waste arguing with your child or repeating the same direction. My programs advocate a power struggle-free policy. There are no winners in a power struggle because someone always feels like the loser. Each battle creates tension anticipating the next interaction, which becomes a new opportunity to battle for control.

Jeopardy Coaching decreases the frequency of arguments because questions displace commands. Questions cleverly neutralize the perceived power differential between child and caregiver, yet you remain in charge. You can still guide while the child retains personal responsibility and power. My clients' parents and the staff at Camp Pegasus notice that this practice leads to fewer power struggles, more cooperation, and much less police work on our part.

Because questions facilitate thought and behavior in the listener, I call this mode of interaction **facilitation**. Facilitation is the opposite of control and direction. Facilitation provides the child the space for and experience of freedom and self-determination. It communicates the child-centered attitude of "I believe in you." You engender confidence in your child's ability to direct his body and life in positive directions.

When your child is regulated and in the Purple and Yellow Phases of Emotional GPS, he can learn and benefit from facilitation questions. He can use his great cognitive capacity to think through the situation and figure out what is expected.

On the other hand, when your child is in distress (Orange Phase) or dysregulated/out-of-control (Red Phase), open-ended questions *escalate* his frustration to rage. During Orange and Red times, you should decrease facilitation and increase direction. This type of guidance is **directive**. In the Orange Phase, you increase your directive-ness (structure) by narrowing your child's options to two acceptable choices. Finally, in the Red Phase, you must become directive and offer the one option: "Your only job is to calm down."

This bears repetition for emphasis: Jeopardy Coaching (Facilitation) is only useful in the Purple and Yellow Phases. It makes things worse in the Orange and Red Phases.

To sum up, let's review the complete social coaching process. Begin with Jeopardy Coaching. Your question stimulates the child to evaluate the environment or check his inner experience. Second, he thinks about the appropriate or better thing to do. Hopefully, he independently performs it. Success! Third, you instantly shift from facilitation to TPR (plus a chip, if appropriate). Let's build on the previous examples:

- Q: "What are you supposed to be doing right now?"

    o   The child looks around the room, sees all the other students, and thinks, "Oh, right, we are supposed to be getting our lunch bags out of our cubbies. I'll go too."

    o   He then blends right in and joins peers in transitioning to lunchtime.

    o   Shift to TPR, "Great thinking, Sam. You are getting your lunch right on time."

- Q: "How does he feel right now? Do you want your friend to feel that way? What can you do to help your friend feel better?"

    o   Your child looks at his peer's face, says, "He looks upset with me. I don't want him to feel sad and think bad things about me."

    o   He says, "I'll apologize and tell him I'll play with him next time."

    o   Shift to TPR, "What a great plan! Great thinking by you. Let me know how it goes."

- "How did that work out for you? What could you do next time to get the grade you want?"

    o Your child thinks, "I wish I did better." In brainstorming with you, he eventually says, "Maybe I can use flash cards and have you quiz me, or maybe I can ask the teacher for help."

    o He tries the flash card strategy and gets a 92%.

    o Shift to TPR: "That was a great idea to change up your study plan. *You* did that, congrats."

- "What would be a great conversation-question to ask here? What else can we learn about your friend's weekend?"

    o Your child thinks of the question words he learned in conversation practice at his social skills group: "Who, what, where, when, why, how … Oh. I've got it."

    o He asks, "*Who* did you see the movie with … Did you like it?"

    o Later, give your child TPR: "Those were great conversation-questions! I could tell that you were thinking really hard to come up with your follow-up question. Keep up the good work."

- "Think for a second … What is your 'Road to Success/Happiness?'"

    o "Your child thinks, "I could take a break or try to compromise with my friend … I think I'll take a break."

    o He takes a break to make sure he calms back down to Purple or Yellow phases. He rejoins the play date and finishes with great flexibility and compromise.

    o You say, "Amazing job calming down. You can finish a super fun visit with your friend. You can do that every time you get frustrated." When the friend leaves, give your child a heap of chips for such strong self-regulation work.

Sometimes, you may offer Jeopardy Coaching, but your child stares at you blankly and doesn't seem to have an answer. Try to resist the urge to rescue your child by providing the answer right away. Wait an extra second or two to allow for processing time. Ask, "Would you like a suggestion?" Consider structuring his thinking by offering a clue or reflecting the current situation. Consider the final bullet point immediately preceding this paragraph. You could reflect what you are seeing (without anger or judgement), "Well … you are acting a bit hyper and you're running around and irritating your friend by not playing anything he wants. What could you do to save the play date?"

In Jeopardy Social Coaching your child maintains his autonomy. Your facilitative questions provide him the responsibility to grapple with social-emotional situations. Your child owns the struggle. He evaluates the situation. Only then can he think of the positive behavior to perform, which gives him the opportunity to execute it. When he effectively thinks through the situation and experiences success, he *owns* the success. Victory is his. Capitalize on the moment with enthusiastic TPR. "*You* did that!" Your child's confidence and true self-esteem multiply. As a bonus you gain more cooperation and consideration of the group/family's needs.

I conclude this section with a disclaimer. This section shares a framework for interaction. Obviously, life isn't as neat as I wrote the above scripts. The ideas here are a starting point and require practice. Your child will throw you curveballs, and we need to improvise all the time. Nevertheless, striving for positive engagement with your child is a worthy cause. I encourage you to try your best to use Jeopardy Coaching as often as possible, and to compassionately forgive yourself if, in a moment of frustration, you lapse into old habits. You are baby-stepping toward new social-coping coaching skills in parallel to your child's growth.

Success-Oriented Instructions Reduce Conflict and Increase Cooperation

You may be thinking: "But Mike, I can't avoid giving directions all day long; my child would never make it out of his room in the morning." I agree. Even during facilitation and reinforcement in the Purple and Yellow Phases, there are times in which you need to give instructions. It's a fact of childhood is that kids are dependent on grown-ups. They need you for caregiving, keeping them on task and on schedule, for safety, sustenance, and for health. You possess big picture thinking and your child does not yet. The younger the child is developmentally, the more dependent he is on you. Therefore, you can't always communicate in facilitative question mode. Sometimes kids simply need to know what is expected, what is next on the schedule, or when you need them to do something for the good of the group/family.

I have found that, at their core, most kids with SECCs desire to know and follow the rules. On the inside, they desperately wish to feel successful. They often have trouble proactively identifying— and then independently initiating—the necessary behavior or task. If you effectively let them know what needs to happen, most of the children with whom I work are only too happy to comply.

Several cognitive challenges inherent in SECCs make it difficult for children to comply promptly. They may:

- Hyper-focus on a preferred activity, causing inattention to your verbal directive

- Have trouble with the executive functions of shifting attention, cognition, energy, and mood states

- Have weak working memory and forget parts two and three of a multi-step direction

- Have auditory processing or receptive language deficits, so spoken instructions may be misunderstood

- Be slow processers, which requires additional time to execute various functions

Those cognitive gaps may cause the child with SECCs to:

- Miss some or all of the verbal directive

- Require multiple reminders/prompts from caregivers

- Forget one or more parts of a multi-step instruction and leave the task incomplete

- Take longer than the neurotypical child to stop what he is doing and complete the task you assign

- Frustrate you, because you expect/need the child to complete the task you are requesting, which leads to inefficiency and large expenditures of energy and attention from you, when you need/wish to attend to another task

At this point I offer a few communication tips to help your child succeed (for the sake of all involved). These tips don't guarantee that your child will leap to action and complete *every* task in record time, but, in my experience, they certainly make a difference. Hopefully, your improved delivery of directions will help him decrease anxiety and stress, comply more easily, decrease your frustration, improve efficiency in your group/family, and promote peaceful interactions.

The beginning and most important step is: *be sure you gain your child's attention before speaking.*

Go to your child and avoid shouting instructions from another room or floor. That may work with other children, but you have no guarantee that your directions land with the child with SECCs. Perhaps he is hyper-focused on an activity and didn't pay attention to your meaning; perhaps he didn't understand your words, or perhaps he had a rough day at school and tunes out your instructions because it feels like yet another demand on his flexibility. From afar you'll never know why you didn't get a response unless you are physically present. You'll only feel frustrated. *Walk to the room where your child is. Be there.* Once there …

Get your child's attention. Call your child's name with a firm clear voice (maybe a few times) until he points his eyes at you. If your child is engaged in a preferred activity, he will probably be in hyper-focus mode, in which all other sensory channels are ignored. He may not hear auditory input. Superficially, it appears that he is ignoring you. I assert that it is not disrespect, but a deep focus to the exclusion of all else. You may need to gently break your child's hyper-focus in order to have him attend to your instructions. Here is how you do it: Place a gentle hand slowly on his shoulder or upper back. Start with the lightest possible pressure as not to completely startle him, and then increase pressure. Simultaneously, say, "Johnny, I see you are watching that video, but I am about to give you important instructions, so I need your eyes." These are alternate ways to request attention: "Please send your eyes to me." "Look away from your screen for a minute." "Check in over here." or "Think about me with your eyes."

Importantly, you should not demand eye *contact*. Don't require eye to eye gaze. That can be overwhelming to the child with CECCs. It is enough if the child looks up from whatever he is doing or looks in your general direction. The combination of your touch (tactile sensory input) and your request for visual attention may interrupt his hypnotic focus long enough for him to attend to your instruction.

Most important, *wait until your child looks at you or otherwise demonstrates attention to you,* then speak your instruction.

Be brief and clear. Too much language confuses our kids. Whether they experience weakness in receptive language, auditory processing, processing speed, or working memory, language can sometimes feel overwhelming and complicated. Once flooded by words or ideas, the child cannot take in any more auditory information, and you are wasting your breath.

- Think about what your main point is before you start speaking. Over-talking makes kids tune out.

- Say what you mean and mean what you say.

- Use the fewest and simplest words possible so your child does not get distracted trying to decode them.

- Avoid idioms, sarcasm, and figurative speech because many of our children are literal and concrete. They don't intuit the larger meaning of these statements and find themselves confused and unsure of how to respond.

- Ask your child to repeat back his understanding of the instruction to confirm accurate understanding of the directions.

- For repeat processes like the morning wake up and school prep or bedtime, publish and post visual schedules and checklists in critical places such as the bedroom, bathroom, or kitchen. For instance, when you direct your child to complete his bedtime routine, instead of micromanaging each step, instruct him to use the checklist to complete all the steps. Then create a Do Rule with a prescribed amount of bonus bucks if he can complete all the steps. For greater structure, add a timer and challenge him to complete the checklist before the timer sounds, and then add TPR plus bucks.

To further promote independence and success, write down multi-step instructions on a sticky pad, note card, or portable dry erase board to aid with memory and follow through. Here is what won't help: Telling your child, "Go upstairs, make your bed, brush your teeth, get dressed, pack up your backpack, and come back down for breakfast." How many of those things do you think will get done? In any situation like this, write, publish, and post a checklist of the steps or tasks involved. Post it in the bathroom and say, "Check in with me when you have completed the whole list." Use TPR and/or tokens to reinforce independent completion of the whole checklist.

Let's anticipate one more challenge to completion of this set of directives: your child's functional awareness of time and limits. Time can feel abstract and seem invisible to the child with SECCs. Your child may get "lost in time" if you give instructions for a task that either has multiple steps or that needs to be completed at a later deadline. The tongue-in-cheek phrase "lost in time" means your child might not be able to manage his time to make steady progress on the tasks. He may get distracted and do a preferred off-task activity, then suddenly rush to complete the assignment, and then blame you. "You didn't give me enough time." Provide an egg timer or a visual timer (like the Time Timer™, available on Amazon) so he can keep track of elapsed time and deadlines. "Let's see if you can finish your list in under fifteen minutes. Can you beat the timer?" The elapsing visual field and gentle beep create a more concrete deadline. (Occasionally a child may feel more anxious and overly pressured by a timer. Know your child and experiment with timers to determine if this helps him succeed.)

Patience. Give your child extra time to process and comply. Your child with SECCs may be slow to cooperate with instructions. In most situations, it is not intentional or personal. He needs extra processing time. His mind is working hard to understand your language and rationale for the request, and he must mentally shift out of his previous activity/mindset. The fast pace of the neurotypical world can be hard for the child with underlying SECCs. One or more cognitive challenges may be at play: slow processing speed, weak working memory, rigid/inflexible thinking, and auditory processing challenges. Don't forget: most kids want to be 'good' and noncompliant behavior is a communication that something is wrong. Use your Iceberg Theory when you experience the child who routinely opposes or defies your directives. What is communicated by the wisdom of the behavior? What does he need? What skill is he missing? Is anything in the environment blocking his cooperation?

Regardless, after you provide instructions the success-oriented way, allow for mental processing and transition time. Do not rush to say, "Come on, Eddie. Eddie, hurry up. Eddie, let's go. You're not listening." Repeated prompts (a.k.a. nagging, in kid terms) create more pressure and a wall of noise so that your child can't even think about cooperating with your actual task. If you would normally wait three seconds before repeating the instruction, hang back and count to seven or ten instead. Try this seven-second exercise to experience what it might be like to give your child more processing time. Count to seven "Mississippi" as follows, "One Mississippi … two Mississippi … three Mississippi … " Pause your reading for a moment and actually do it right now; pay attention to how long a seven-count really feels. It's quite the pregnant pause, right?

If you allow seven to ten seconds after your child hears your directive, you may be surprised that he actually does what you asked. He might transition from his last task, coordinate his body movements, and start executing. Notice and immediately shift to TPR. "Great listening!" Or, "Thank you for your great cooperation." Offer chips to reinforce the excellent choice and cooperative effort.

Sometimes children don't comply because they don't understand your words. This can happen to bright children with wonderful vocabularies. Patiently ask your child to repeat back his understanding of the instruction. Say, "Just to make sure you got it, repeat back what you understand the directions to be." Be ready to rephrase the direction. If you repeat the exact same words, your child's comprehension might not improve. Communication is a sloppy, imperfect affair. You may think you were crystal clear, but your message might not land. Harness your strong desire for your child to understand and comply. That will help you find the patience to re-explain your point in different words.

Some noncompliance occurs because the child doesn't like what you are asking him to do. He may ask you, "But why? Why do I have to do it? Why? Why *now*?" To start, please know that many children with SECCs are "logic kids," which means they need things to make logical sense. When peers' requests, certain rules, or adult requests don't make sense within the child's own internal system of logic, it is hard for him to cooperate. He finds it difficult even to muster motivation or energy to comply. It's not his fault! In this case it's not a sign of laziness or disrespect. It isn't a character flaw or something you should take personally. When your child asks, "Why?" he is requesting an explanation. You dutifully answer, only to have him ask again. "But why?" You answer again.

If you are familiar with this dynamic and you find yourself exhausted from answering seven to ten "why" questions, I propose a strategy you may love. In this case, your child's "Why" is more than a question. It is also a protest against the reality your child doesn't like. "Why must there be so much hunger in the world? *Why*?" Kids who struggle with advanced math ask over and over, "Why do I have to do this algebra? I'll never use it in my real life. *Why*?" They don't want an actual answer the 176th time they protest with "*Why*?" "Why" is a complaint (and sometimes a tool to drive you crazy).

Here's the antidote for the child who badgers you with "Why?" Proactively W.P.P. a "Rule of 3" structure. It's not a punishment; it's a limit and boundary. The next time you give an instruction to your "logic kid," you will surely be asked your first "Why?"

- Answer once to satisfy the logic kid's need for understanding of the rationale behind the directive.

- After the next "why?" *rephrase* your answer a second time to ensure understanding. Don't use the exact same words as the first request. That is now strike two, as you've explained the request in two different ways.

- Confirm your child's comprehension, "Got it? Repeat back your understanding of what I just said." Once your child confirms understanding, you are no longer responsible to explain.

- The next "Why?" is number three, and you shift from explaining to setting a boundary on the badgering, "I'm not discussing it anymore. You know what you have to do." Provide empathy for the emotion beneath the iceberg and end the questioning. "I know you don't like it, but you just need to do it." "It's hard, but I know you can be flexible and handle this."

If your instructions are for a task that doesn't need to happen immediately, request a time commitment for its completion. "When will you get it done?" "What time can I expect this to be completed?" There is another sneaky way to communicate it by offering an acceptable forced choice, "You can do it now or after dinner. What sounds better to you?" This way of prompting has a built-in expectation that it definitely *will* get accomplished, offering no outs. With forced acceptable choice your child no longer is deciding whether or not to cooperate. Cooperation is a given, it's a matter of *when*.

As always, offer TPR and reward behaviors like asking for clarification, persistence on a difficult task, problem-solving obstacles that initially block task completion, and independent accomplishment of preliminary steps such as gathering necessary materials or information.

Assume an Educational and Social-Coaching Stance

Every behavior that your child performs reveals his abilities and/or weaknesses. Any time an activity progresses or goes well, it reveals your child's ability. Conversely, any social error your child performs reveals a weaker social or coping skill. Over time, you'll notice patterns of social challenges that enable you to predict future challenges. "I know he's going to have a hard time at the miniature golf birthday party because he withdrew and didn't socialize at the last two unstructured parties at the bowling alley and the pool." How your child copes with any process reveals how he approaches most processes.

On the path of social growth, there are stumbles, turns, and bumps. In any learning process, people make mistakes before they achieve mastery. In the Purple and Yellow phases, your child is still regulated and in control. In those phases social mess-ups provide moments ripe for incidental teaching and learning. Each social miscue reveals an underlying gap in social understanding, problem solving, or calming skills. Your job is to peer beneath the iceberg and make your best guess which cognitive skill gap caused the problem.

For example, if your child cries and shuts down every time the piano teacher provides a constructive correction, note that behavior and assess the skill gap. You might define it as your child struggling to tolerate making a mistake, because it makes him feel embarrassed, imperfect, or out of control. You may infer from that one incident that your child has not yet developed frustration tolerance, or that he has unrealistically high expectations for himself, "I mustn't make a mistake (perfectionism)."

What then? How can you coach your child? He already feels as though he is in a negative feedback loop with the world. You might worry that one more correction from you could make him feel bad or push him into Orange or Red Phases.

As a reminder, you shouldn't do social-emotional coaching during those phases. In those moments, your child's brain is overwhelmed with emotion and is not open to coaching. Let the Emotional GPS guide your support. Later, when your child is in the Purple or Yellow phases, you might broach the topic.

Fill In the Cognitive Gaps

First, you need to identify the missing or underdeveloped skill or awareness. Your goal is to help your child prevent the noncompliance or meltdown from happening the next time and beyond. Your child benefits from understanding the big-picture truth that he is only human, and all humans are imperfect. Another truth is that it is normal to make mistakes when you learn and practice new things. The fact of the matter is, with practice, we get better at things.

Perhaps your child thinks you might be disappointed in his mistakes. Here, you could clarify expectations that you are less concerned with him getting everything right and more interested in him practicing positive habits like hard work and perseverance. You could also take a different tack: you may want to teach and rehearse breathing techniques to keep calm in the face of correction and frustration. These are all completely valid and worthy things to work on. I want to reassure you that there is rarely just one correct skill to build. Don't put pressure on yourself to select the perfect response or solution. You can absolutely check your gut suspicion by running it by your child, "I was wondering if you were refusing to practice because you worry that you have to be perfect or that a mistake means you stink at piano. What do you think?" Pick a skill that makes sense, corroborate it with your child and run with it.

Finally, when your child demonstrates the new coping strategy you brainstormed together, catch, praise, and give sloppy TPR. Load up on the chips to celebrate the breakthrough. Give yourself credit too for staying engaged with the process! Let's break down a sample social coaching process.

Be Curious: What Does this Iceberg Behavior Mean?

The Wisdom of The Behavior is that it always communicates what's really going on for your child. Wise social coaches ask the following questions. What's beneath the surface? What is the wisdom of the behavior? What did the child really *need*, not merely want? What weaker social-coping skill may have led to the social faux pas? The following are six scripts you might try:

- Ask, "Is this how you wanted it to turn out? How did you want things to go?" or

- Ask, "What were you thinking when … ?" Or, "What were you feeling when … ?" or

- Ask, "What is happening for you right now?"

- Ask, "What made this hard/extra hard for you today?"

- Ask, "Is there anything realistic that I can do or change to make this easier for you?"

- Ask, "What is one small thing you can do differently next time to avoid what just happened?"

When to Intervene? Hang Back Until You Can't

Remember Targeted Ignoring? Deciding when to coach your child is possibly the most challenging balancing act for any caregiver. "I thought you told me to use Targeted Ignoring and focus on the positive? Now I'm confused." I wish the answer were cut and dry. There is a little grey in between always or never intervening. As a guideline for you, there are three things that should cause you to leap into action.

1. Impact: Directly and negatively impacting someone else

2. Function: Behavior blocking functionality and productivity

3. Dysregulation: Loss of emotional control and safety

Pick your battles carefully. Because we use Targeted Ignoring for most negative events and we determinedly attend to the positive, you need a quick and easy way to determine when to reflect and when to coach.

Micromanaging and coaching each and every little social error is exhausting for all parties and defeating for your child. Furthermore, helicopter coaching breeds dependence on you, but you want your child to practice age-appropriate independence. You want him to have the responsibility to strengthen his social cognition muscle. You want him to solve his own problems and self-regulate. Therefore, you must intervene *judiciously*.

The rule of thumb is to first hang back, observe, and TPR—until events force you to intervene. Let's say your child has a play date disagreement with a friend. The friend is bored with working on crafts together and wants to transition to playing board games. Your child wants to continue crafting.

In the Art of Friendship model, you should stay on the sidelines and observe. Observation is not disengagement. You are not outside gardening. Rather, you privately root for your child to recover and rescue the situation himself. You are like an on-call firefighter.

The children are debating and negotiating. Occasionally one voice or the other flares up in volume, but they are still working on a compromise. "How about if we finish this project in ten minutes then play something else?" Or, "What if we keep doing this project and then make some slime?" You might even call over to them with encouraging TPR, "I love how you two are working hard to work it out! Keep compromising!" You determine that their negotiations are still productive, reciprocal, and certainly not destructive (to their friendship). This sounds like the two kids are in the Yellow Phase, in which they can still problem solve. Kudos to you for letting things play out.

As the process winds on, the children appear to hit an impasse. You hear voices rise. One is yelling, "You never want to do what I want to do!" Your child hollers, "If you don't do crafts with me then we're not friends anymore!" You hear blame, ultimatums, rigid declarations, and rising anger. It sounds like they are in the Orange Phase of distress. Not out of control yet, problem-solving ability has shrunk to a minimum. Feelings are hurt, and now the play date—and possibly the friendship—is at risk. At this moment, it is obvious that the conversation is no longer *productive or functional*. You should swoop in swiftly, "Hey you two. Hold on a minute. It sounds like you're having a hard time working something out and now you're mad. (reflection of the process)." Offer an acceptable choice (Orange Phase support): "I'm not saying you need to work this out this second. Would you like a break from each other in different rooms or would you like a snack? (acceptable choice)." When cooler heads prevail, you can return to coaching. "So, sounds like you both wanted different things. Now that things are calmed down, how can you work everything out?" Then negotiations can continue.

Personal Emotional Impact: The first determining factor for your intervention is whether a social behavior *directly impacts a person, family, or group*. If so, then you should rush to coach. You can tell when your child's behavior affects individuals if a peer or sibling is upset, crying, or offended. If you hear urgent protests of, *"Hey!"* or *"Stop!"* clearly, one child or the other has lost patience. If an all-out Red Phase war erupts, separate the two children with your Red Phase directive: "Both of you…*pause*…separate *now*. You are upset. Your only job is to calm down."

On the other hand, if a peer seems unmoved and ignores your child's behavior and the moment passes, it is okay to let the faux pas go. Targeted ignoring requires you to let it go. There was no personal emotional impact.

In a peer group situation, hang back and observe whether the group can wrestle with the conflict and handle it themselves. Does your child adjust his behavior? Does he compromise? Does he walk away and take a break? Those are small victories that need to be validated with TPR (and possibly bucks). First, observe if your child and the peer(s) are conflicting but *still negotiating somewhat productively*. Even mildly frustrated tones are acceptable if productive discussion is happening. The following are cues you should look for that indicate that your intervention is required:

- Your child is one-sidedly arguing or dominating a peer

- The exchange has escalated to out-and-out yelling

- One or both kids perseverate on the same solution and go 'round and 'round with no resolution

- Escalating volume, name-calling, or physical hurting such as shoving, hitting, kicking, or biting

It's time to swoop in.

Function: The second green light to intervene is guided by the question of *functionality*. Ask yourself, "Is this working for the group or not working?" "Can I ignore or modify the child's behavior in order for us to do what we have to do?" If the behavior makes the process impossible, quite literally, it's *non-functional*. It's not working, it's time to intervene.

In a structured group situation like camp or school, disruptive behaviors may prevent an adult leader from teaching or instructing. You have points to make and you need the group to hear your message. It's for their benefit. You can't have disruptions, but in these cases, the group's process is obstructed by the child's behavior. It's time to swoop in.

Dysregulation: Lastly, intervention is required when your child with SECCs is *dysregulated and/or behaving unsafely*. The most compassionate and loving thing you can do is to step in with support. Aside from the potential risk of injury or destruction of property, children hate to lose control. It feels rotten and embarrassing, especially in the aftermath when the child regains composure and cognitive ability. "I can't believe I did that." Certainly, if your child is prone to Red Phase loss of self-control, you want to keep vigilant. If your child is showing Orange Phase behavior, head it off before he crashes into the Red Phase.

Some signs a child is in the Orange Phase:

- Sudden non-compliance

- Shouting a guttural "Aargh."

- Hands balled up into fists

- Leg pumping

- Gritting teeth

- Rocking

- Ripping paper

- Throwing unsafe objects

- Loud voice and pressured speech; whining

- Extra-inflexible, demanding or blaming

- Chatty child growing silent

- Arguing

- Name-calling

- Threatening

Supporting the Individual Child Who is Struggling

This is a reminder that Yellow Phase is mild frustration and needs only casual facilitation. Caregivers should move in gently with curiosity and trust that the child's mental apparatus can figure out this situation. Strike a facilitative stance with reflection and Jeopardy Coaching:

- **Step 1:** Ask: "What's happening?"

- **Step 2:** If no response, reflect what you see and label the underlying feeling, not the behavior. "You look frustrated." or "You look disappointed."

- **Step 3:** Open-ended problem solving: "How do you want to handle this?" Wait and allow the child to suggest kid-level solutions. Kid-level solutions are often creative and not necessarily what you would think of first. "I could activate my force shield so his insults don't hurt my feelings." That's great and should be applauded with TPR: "Awesome solution, Tommy. You handled it!"

If the child moves to Orange Phase distress, pause demands/expectations briefly, "You look stressed out right now. You don't have to keep trying _____." Then narrow from open-ended problem solving to an acceptable choice in question form. Ask:

- "Do you want to take a break on the carpet or take a walk to the water fountain?"

- "Can you come up with a "Rescue Thought" or make this "No Biggie"?" (cognitive coping skills language for frustration tolerance)

- "Do you want to keep trying to work on this or come back to it later?"

Hang back and watch your child cope. Give him the gift of responsibility for his own problem solving. When he does cope, revert right back to strong TPR and a handful of tokens. "Excellent job dealing with that! You avoided the Red Phase and got back to Yellow."

If your child does not cope, he may tip into the Red Phase. I know you wish it didn't happen, and it's truly unfortunate. Remembering the Child-Centered Frame, he's doing his best to function at his best at every given moment, limited by skill gaps and factors like hunger or tiredness. The meltdown moment was simply too overwhelming for your child's coping skills. It's not his fault or preference. His only job is to calm down now, and problem solving will have to wait until afterward.

Conflict Resolution for Multiple Children

Common disagreements can turn to arguments due to inflexibility and weak problem-solving skills. When your child becomes stuck in an argument with peers, the social coaching stance is that it is a learning opportunity. A big part of you may feel impatient to resume peace by solving the problem for the combatants. Be aware of these urges. That will permit you to take a breath, slow down the process, and let the conflict resolution begin.

Yellow Phase Conflict: Kids Go First

Our default social training stance is to offer independence, TPR, and bucks, in that order. When a disagreement happens, attempt to let the children try to handle it. You may be right near the arguers or you may be at a distance. Hang back and ascertain whether their communication is productive. If it is, they are managing the mild frustration that naturally occurs when two people disagree.

Notice your inner experience to help you hang back. You may feel tension or anxiety rise in your gut, anticipating that arguing will escalate. Note your anxiety, which could stimulate an impulse to act prematurely. If their voices remain at relatively Yellow Phase levels and they are still offering alternative solutions, don't intercede. Let them own their relationship and their struggle. When they arrive at a mutually agreeable kid-level solution they *own* their own success.

Positively reflect the *process*. "I love how you are still trying to work this out." "It's great that you are not giving up on compromising." If they successfully work it out, give gushy TPR and bonus chips to bring attention to the success. Reinforce it for the two negotiators and model the successful social skill for other children in earshot.

Orange Phase Conflict: Caregivers First

If the negotiation turns into an argument and you observe angry faces and raised voices, move in quickly, because kids often escalate to anger quickly. If the children get stuck repeating the same inflexible solutions without compromise, and if the tone changes from collaborating to hollering and insulting, it is time to intervene. Pause demands and offer an acceptable choice, in that order.

There's another guidepost that you may use to leap into supportive action. If *you* grow irritable and can't take it anymore, you've waited too long. You should assist *before* your blood starts boiling. An angry you probably won't give your best coaching performance. Your self-awareness can tell you when to jump in. Bottom line: The moment the communication becomes unproductive or destructive, swoop in quickly and call a time out. "Hold on. Hold on here. Time out. I'm not saying…"

Rules of engagement for Orange Phase conflict intervention:

- Let the arguers know they are not in trouble.

- You must not play judge and jury. Don't take a side and dictate the outcome. To kids, it feels like you're picking a winner and loser, or worse, who you like better or worse. To a child, once it turns into winning/losing more/less favorite, no learning occurs! If you pick a winner and a loser, everyone loses because you have increased the rivalry. Losers resent you. They also resent the "winner" and may want to exact revenge later. (The only exception to the guideline of not playing judge is when a child breaks a safety rule or is obviously verbally attacking someone.) Instead …

- Let both kids know that each will get to say their entire opinion without being interrupted. "You both will have a chance to talk."

- If the argument disrupts an entire class/group, someone needs to pull the combatants aside and allow the lesson/activity to continue. Pulling the arguers aside prevents other group members from getting angry at them for holding up the process and prevents shaming of kids receiving social coaching.

Conflict Resolution Script for Two or More Kids

- Ask, "What's happening here?" Give each child a chance to state his position.

- Ask both kids, "How does this make your feel?" (Develop emotion awareness of self and other.)

- Have each child repeat back his understanding of the other's feelings and statements for empathy and understanding. "So you are saying that _____happened, and you feel hurt, and you say _____happened, and you feel _____. I got it." After confirming that they heard each other …

- Move to problem solving. "What can the two of you do to get back to _____?"

- Other cueing statements are as follows (Art of Friendship social skills and assertiveness language are italicized):

  o "What did you want at that time?"

  o "Stick up for yourself—nicely … Use your *Power of I.* Say: I want _____."

o   "You are stuck. You can get unstuck by saying, "How about we _____.""

o   "Can you be *bendy* (flexible) and compromise?"

o   "What are two ways that you can compromise?"

o   "What would it look like if you mixed your ideas together in the *idea pot*?"

o   "How could you *balance the scales of fun* and take turns?"

o   "If you changed your mind, what new idea would you suggest?"

o   Offer a "Do Over."

Three-Level Learning

Children's conflicts can be healthy when they don't become destructive. Constructive disagreements involve listening and hearing one another's perspectives and compromising when possible. Frustration and anger may be OK if the participants refrain from acting out on each other. Conflict becomes destructive when things turn unkind or hurtful.

When you step in to coach children through conflict, begin with a judgment-free attitude. Conflict behavior isn't bad behavior. As always, it is critical that you activate your self-awareness. Are you feeling impatient, frustrated, disappointed, or ashamed? Feelings like those may cause you to rush in to rescue, lecture, or punish. Use your knowledge of SECCs for empathy.

Theory of Mind is the cognitive awareness and acceptance that different people have different thoughts, feelings, and motivations. A conflict reveals both participants' inner workings. A conflict happens when two minds with differing thoughts bump into each other and the combatants don't know how to handle the bumping. If an argument escalates and grows destructive, it reveals a lack of flexibility, lack of self-regulation, and prolonged egocentrism (the need to be correct). Perhaps it also shows weaker problem-solving or assertiveness skills. As always, the argument unveils a skill deficit that needs remediation. Your empathic inner monologue would sound something like this: "It's not his fault. He can't help it because he doesn't have the skills to negotiate disagreements."

Children can learn a lot from conflict resolution:

- **Functionality: getting back on track.** Get back to fun and function by working it out. The very act of working through and resolving a conflict proves to the child something he didn't trust, that conflict resolution is possible. Each time a child resolves a disagreement, be sure to validate with TPR so he encodes that memory. "Incredible job working that out. Do that again next time you have a disagreement."

- **Success: repetition for mastery and confidence.** Build a library of memories proving that successful conflict resolution is possible for your child. Recurrent practice of negotiation and compromise helps him memorize those skills until they become habit. Using Jeopardy Coaching you might ask, "How about we call a do-over." "Let's just agree to disagree." Or, "Why don't we compromise?" Each time your child solves a social problem, be sure to TPR, "*You* did that!"

- **Emotional awareness: developing Theory of Mind.** Children can improve real-time identification of the emotion that is triggered during disagreements. When you reflect what you see, the child sees his own frustration. Over time your child may develop the ability to notice peers' body language and tone of voice. "Hold on you two, look at each other's faces right now. Are you happy with each other? Do you want Mark to feel upset? Mark, do you want Stephen to be mad? How can the two of you work this out and get back to fun? Would you like to take a quick break from one another to cool down? You can always come back together when you get back to the Purple Phase."

Emotion awareness enables the individual to self-regulate and make better choices. Understanding the other person's perspective also begins mutual problem solving.

All of this develops problem-solving skills that result in prevention of future conflicts: Breaking up a conflict is not proactive; it's reactive. You react after tempers flare. An argument is pointless and non-productive if your child does not learn from it.

At the conclusion of each conflict resolution/problem-solving process, have your child or children make a plan for the future. Develop a plan of action, and the fight you broke up suddenly makes the future better.

When the conflict is over and peace reigns again, try to use the social breakdown to prevent similar ones in the future. Have the child brainstorm for a preventive solution. End the coaching conversation by asking, "If this were to happen again, what do you think you might say or do to avoid _____ again?" To strengthen the proactive plan, write and publish the solution as a reminder of the great learning that occurred. Wouldn't it be cool to keep a "solution book" for each child with his plans? The child with SECCs can keep a log of all the life lessons and plans he makes, like his own social manual.

THINK → FEEL → DO

THE PROBLEM SOLVER'S WORKSHEET

1. What new way can I THINK about it?

Maybe...

If I were bendy and flexible...

Well at least...

Sometimes...

Different kids have different minds...

2. How will I FEEL with my new thought?

Solve the Problem.

3. What are 2-3 things I can DO?

1. _____
2. _____
3. _____

Let it go. I can't control it.

What would be a better way to get what I want?

4. TRY IT!

☺

PURPLE PHASE

TAKE THE ROAD TO HAPPINESS/ SUCCESS

What happened?

What did I want?

What did I THINK?

I MUST...

I'll NEVER...

Only MY way...

He/She HAS TO...

My thoughts made me FEEL:

What did I DO?

☹

RED PHASE

ROAD TO ANGER/ SADNESS/ STRUGGLE

Name: _____

88

Structured Problem Solving: The Think-Feel-Do Problem Solving Worksheet

Structured problem solving helps children in many ways. For the child who is a concrete thinker or who is new to the social coaching process, problem solving on paper has numerous benefits.

Our problem-solving worksheet graphically walks the child through the thoughts, feelings, and actions that led to the conflict or problem. Then, on the same paper, it shows the child a new path. The child, with your guidance, can fill in new, helpful ways of thinking and new, helpful behaviors for the situation you are reviewing. On the Think-Feel-Do Problem-Solving Worksheet, the child sees that he has a choice in directing his life in powerfully positive ways.

Children see and understand that they can choose the outcome they want (self-determination). The problem-solving worksheet visually echoes the Art of Friendship decision-making lesson called "The Road to Happiness," and literally shows the child's path back to success.

Working on paper creates emotional distance from the pain attached to the experience. Sitting face to face with an adult to autopsy a social mishap can be shaming. Admitting, "I messed up in the following way." places your child in a very vulnerable position. Externalizing a solution process onto paper projects the mishap "over there" and "outside of me" which makes problem solving much less threatening. There is no way to avoid problem-solving social goofs, but you can make it less painful with this tool.

The completed worksheet becomes a permanent record of the solution. It can be saved and posted on a wall or your refrigerator as a reminder for the next challenge. Teachers can hold it, or you may slip it inside your child's desk at school as a reminder. Permanence also allows you to monitor progress with your child. Review a worksheet from five months ago and celebrate just how far your child has progressed.

Lastly, the Think-Feel-Do form is a whole-brain solution. This worksheet uses language and writing (left brain hemisphere), but also uses colors, shapes, creativity, and a visual sequence (right brain hemisphere). When both hemispheres of the brain are used, it is called a "whole brain approach," which is known to improve memory encoding and retrieval.

The Think-Feel-Do Problem-Solving Worksheet borrows well-known concepts from the cognitive-behavioral approach to therapy (CBT). Here is the quick background:

- We all have immediate, automatic thoughts related to our experiences. We may or may not always be aware of these sudden, beneath-the-surface thoughts.

- Those thoughts lead to feelings (body sensations and tensions)—some subtle, some strong.

- Feelings spark impulses to act.

Thought leads to feeling, which leads to action. Think-Feel-Do. T-F-D. Most people are unaware of this automatic and invisible cycle. It is more magnified in people who struggle with emotional-behavioral challenges. By becoming aware of one's T-F-D cycle one can develop self- control. It is possible to develop better control over emotions and impulses by unlocking the secrets of T-F-D.

In terms of emotion and behavior management, we can learn to control only two of those three items. Let's rule out what we can't control, the 'F' in T-F-D. We can't control our feelings through sheer force of will. Sure, you may be able to hold them in temporarily, but they always seek an outlet. The truth is, you can't stop feeling what you feel because feelings are activated directly by automatic and sometimes subconscious thoughts. An event happens in your environment and you have a reaction. Occasionally you are aware of stronger and clear thought-signals from your mind. More often, the immediate thought is a fleeting stealth notion that you don't consciously notice.

If you can't control your 'F', you can learn to gain more awareness and self-determination of your 'T' and 'D'. There are two things we can learn to modify and control. We can learn new realistic and helpful ways to think about the world and we can learn and plan positive new actions (behaviors). The Think-Feel-Do Problem-Solving Worksheet is a tool to help your child become aware of his T-F-D and improve control of the two elements that are controllable. With improved awareness and control, your child can take corrective action to ensure that the social-coping mishap doesn't happen again.

Handling Inevitable Avoidance of the Think-Feel-Do Problem-Solving Worksheet

It is not necessary to use the worksheet for *every* social-coaching situation. Most children seem to want to avoid all problem-solving conversations for fear that they will be ashamed or punished. It feels *bad* to revisit a defeat. If your child makes initial expressions of wanting to postpone the social coaching conversation, you might negotiate with him once or twice. If his "postponement" becomes a pattern, it may belie deeper avoidance, which is an impediment to social growth. By delaying, your child hopes that you will simply forget about it. Instead, you need to hold him accountable and have the conversation at the rescheduled time. Reschedule the coaching conversation. "When will we talk about this? It needs to be later tonight or tomorrow. You decide." "Let's set a specific time, say 3:30, or after dinner?"

If your child argues or flatly refuses the problem-solving worksheet, you have a problem on your hands. It does not help matters if you get frustrated and yell and scream, lecture or punish. That proves to the child that coaching conversations are overwhelming. Your child will grow the best if you place the responsibility and control on him.

Because your child won't grow without social coaching conversations, they are as critical as eating or sleeping. Fret not when you meet resistance. There is an answer if you leverage your adult authority at home or school. Once you identify your child's pattern of resistance or refusal, consider proactive use of the "forced break" or "grounding" strategy. This strategy uses an 'If-Then', action-reaction formula such as, "*If* you don't participate in collaborative coaching conversations, *then* you lose privileges."

While on a forced break, your child should not do anything other than homework. There should be no gaming, texting, or other preferred activities. Allow your child to be bored. For a more detailed description of this approach to building your child's responsibility and accountability, please see the upcoming section in Chapter 5, "Deal Breakers: The Child's Plan versus The Family Plan, Forced Breaks, and Grounding."

In a calm, firm voice, state the expectation that, "These coaching conversations are really important. They are here to help you get along better and succeed more often. If you don't want to work on the problem-solving worksheet, that's your choice, but if you refuse, from now on *you are also choosing* to shut yourself down. You will have a break/be grounded until you complete the Think-Feel-Do worksheet. I'll be happy to help you if you want."

Using the Worksheet

Depending on your child's developmental level and degree of independence, you may need to walk him through each step of the worksheet. You may begin with the bottom half, which reviews the thoughts, feelings, and actions your child went through on his way to the social/behavioral mistake. If he is extremely sensitive and feels hurt by reviewing the process that led to the unhelpful behavior, you can be flexible, skip the bottom sequence, and begin with the upper path with the circles.

Next, for the top half, you need to help the child come up with replacement Think-Feel-Do's. "If this exact situation were to happen again, what would you do differently?" Ask your child the sequential questions on the top half of the page, from left to right, traveling up the "Road to Happiness." If possible, have him write in the blanks with new, adaptive ways to think, feel, and behave in the situation.

The fact that a feeling is generated by a thought and not in your child's control should be a point of emphasis in your coaching. Always point out that the feeling inevitably follows the thought. Reveal the thought error when reviewing the lower path that leads to the mistake. Then, highlight the automatic positive feeling and behavior that arise when your child intentionally practices a realistic/helpful thought.

Help your child see that the new replacement Think-Feel-Do is within his power, because he can control two out of the three steps on his Road to Happiness.

- "If you think _____, then you feel _____.

- Then, when you feel that way, it is way easier for you to do _____."

- Wish your child luck, and say, "Next time _____ happens, I can't wait to notice how well you handle it!"

CHAPTER 5

THERAPEUTIC LOVE: SETTING LIMITS FOR UNACCEPTABLE BEHAVIORS

Love and positivity are immensely important in social-emotional coping skills training. None of that is possible if a child feels or behaves out of control. When children lose control over emotions or impulses, they can't absorb your positivity. In all pre-Red Phases, your child can make positive decisions and behavior can be taught and shaped. Different than Red Phase behaviors, "Deal Breakers" are behaviors that are simply unacceptable and unworkable.

Remember, when your child is in the Red Phase, we need to compassionately allow her nervous system to regain peace. Hurting others verbally or physically are the most obvious examples of pre-Red Deal Breakers. Other unsafe or risky behaviors also fit this term, such as elopement (running away) or impulsively dangerous behaviors (climbing too high).

Lastly, some behaviors are unacceptable and completely non-functional for a family or group. These include pervasive oppositional and defiant behavior. Nonfunctional behaviors such as these include:

- Defiance and complete refusal to cooperate with adult directives

- Pervasive refusal to participate in social coaching or give effort on the Think-Feel-Do Problem Solving Worksheet

These last two behaviors completely block your child from academic and social-emotional improvement and success. As always, it's essential to explore beneath the iceberg to figure out triggers to these behaviors.

Aside from the disruptiveness of refusal, defiance, and non-participation in coaching, the child loses psychologically as well. Let's take a brief peek at emotional and impulse control—and the consequences of the child imposing defiant control.

A Holding Environment

All children must have the abiding sense that "my caregivers can keep me safe and handle my most intense moments." It's as essential as oxygen for your child's success. Here's why:

Let's start at the beginning. Newborn babies feel safe, secure, and internally regulated when they are swaddled. We wrap them up tight and they (usually) cry less as their nervous systems get used to feeling safe. Swaddling provides containment and structure, so their floppy little limbs don't dangle wildly. *People of all ages need to feel safe and secure.* Children and adolescents still need varying amounts of "swaddling," in the form of a metaphoric "container" for their feelings and impulses. The therapy profession calls this emotional container a "holding environment."

Children are "held" or "swaddled" with rules, expectations, guidelines, and adult supervision and guidance. For example, consider a fifth-grade class. With the strict and firm homeroom teacher, the children are well behaved. The same group of students behaves much more wildly in the science classroom, where the teacher is known to be unstructured and accommodating. Clear expectations with explicit and predictable responses ("if-then" consequences) are a holding environment. Rules, expectations, and supervision with limits provide the "swaddling" older children require.

Different people require different amounts of "holding." As a rule, the younger the child, the more structure is required, but we still need to individualize. Children who are sedentary rule followers need less strong rules and consequences. Compare them with the impulsive child who tests limits and usually seeks novel stimulation. Individuals who have weaker internal controls need a stronger container than the highly controlled individual. For children with SECCs, regardless of chronological age, the self-control and mental organization parts of the brain may be immature relative to their peers. They may need stronger, clearer, and more overt structure to feel good and succeed.

Children need to know exactly what is expected in each setting they enter. If a child does not intuitively pick up unwritten situational expectations, then a concrete publication of rules, schedules, and consequences guides her social-coping practice and behavior. Publishing rules, expectations, and schedules makes them real. Make sure you print and post rules, schedules, and consequences. To be crystal clear, I reiterate that *consequences* does not always mean punishment in a teaching and learning philosophy. I'll elaborate as you read on.

Clear Expectations: W.P.P. the Top 3-5 "Decrease-Behavior" Rules- with Positive Replacement Behaviors

When parents and teachers with whom I consult reach this point in the training, they challenge me. "Wait a minute, we can't be ultra-positive every minute of the day." "We can't do targeted ignoring for hitting, insulting peers, defiance, or disruptive behaviors." "We can't just ask Jeopardy questions if my student is constantly interrupting class."

Parents and caregivers who make these points are one hundred percent correct. Some behaviors are absolute Deal Breakers. They are unacceptable and they do impact others' feelings, learning, boundaries, and sense of safety. Targeted ignoring is inappropriate here; action is required.

You know your child's most common—and most likely—violations. Polite requests to stop doing habitual deal-breakers obviously won't work. Yelling is reactive and only makes things worse. If the solution were as simple as a carefully worded request there wouldn't be a need for books like this. Be proactive and anticipate your child's predictable miscues by writing and publishing the top three to five behaviors you want your child to stop doing or do less. These are called **Decrease-Behaviors**. When you draft your Decrease-Behavior list, begin each rule/guideline with the word "No," like this:

- No talking back, just say, "okay" or "I hear you."

- No hitting or kicking; walk away and take a break/ask a grown up for help

- No going in your brother's room without permission; ask first

- No badgering parents with requests; after you ask the same question the third time, the conversation will end and you will need to write it down in your list of "wants"

- No lying; tell the truth and we will work everything out. Lying gets you a bigger consequence than whatever the truth would have been

Notice that when I listed Decrease-Behaviors, I included a positive replacement behavior so your child has *a helpful substitute action to target* while avoiding the negative. Be sure to let her know what positive behavior you expect instead of the prohibited one. Okay, so now you have the Decrease-Behaviors listed. How do you enforce them?

Predictable Logical Consequences

Many children with SECCs aren't aware of the impact of their behavior on individuals and groups. Weakness in reading social cues means that kids with SECCs misinterpret the feedback loop from the environment. If you can't determine from others whether your behavior was received positively or negatively, you won't know whether to persist or change your behavior. For the benefit of impulse control and social development, it is crucial to intentionally teach children if-then, cause-and-effect thinking. Kids can learn accountability and self-responsibility; it starts by over-teaching statements such as:

- "If you do 'X,' then 'Y' happens." "For every *if* there is a *then*."

- "If you do _____ then _____ will happen."

- "If you choose to do ____[inappropriate behavior]____, then you will have _____ consequence."

In the Art of Friendship Social-Coping Curriculum® you will find a few social lessons that reinforce the if-then relationship of action-reaction. Please write up your own social-coping lesson, then teach and post it.

Predictable logical consequences are only to be used for Decrease-Behaviors. They are not effective in teaching positive replacement behaviors. Predictable logical consequences are actionable, direct interventions that inform a child that a certain behavior is not okay and not to be repeated. They are only one part of a teaching and learning process that occurs over time. (Don't forget to understand the wisdom of the behavior underneath the iceberg, empathic reflection, social-coping skill instruction, and TPR + chips.)

All children make mistakes when they are learning, and your child may make the same behavioral error multiple times. She may need to receive the same consequence several times before she recognizes the pattern. When your daughter experiences a predictable logical consequence (or several, if necessary), the message is, "You have self-determination. You choose whether you want to experience this unpleasant consequence. If you don't want the negative outcome to happen again, then *you* are responsible for selecting a positive replacement behavior. Take the Road to Happiness."

The simplest way to plan a predictable logical consequence is to separate the child from the object/person they are not "using" responsibly. Announce and publish rules in the if-then format:

- **If** you don't turn off the iPad when asked, **then** you lose it for the rest of the day.

- **If** you make a mess/break something, **then** you need to fix it or work to pay for its repairs.

- **If** you two keep arguing whether the ball was out of bounds, **then** you will have to sit out and figure it out while the rest of the class gets back to playing. (It's not fair to hold up the whole class from gym.)

- **If** you don't stop insulting your sister, **then** you will be separated and have to spend seven minutes in a different room.

- **If** you keep arriving at home well past your curfew, **then** you won't be able to take the car out next weekend.

Consequences must be *predictable*. They must be given when they are anticipated, pre-announced, and published. Kids always find new and creative ways to let us know that they haven't quite internalized a skill. If a child with SECCs engages in a significant behavioral miscue but no rule or expectation about it exists, it is not fair to jump to a punishment. That's like changing the rules in the middle of a game, *not fair*.

When your child unveils a new deal-breaker that didn't yet have an explicit No-Rule, you need to have a coaching discussion. In it, you should explain to the child what the unwritten expectation *was*. Second, you need to make sure she learns how it impacts others and what's in it for her (socially, academically, etc.) to follow the unwritten rule. Finally, you should W.P.P. a new Decrease-Behavior rule and collaborate with your child to create the accompanying positive replacement behavior. After all those expectations are set, you can say, "This rule/skill is so important that we are creating a special bonus chip deal whenever you do the Positive Replacement Behavior."

Deal Breakers: The Child's Plan Versus The Family Plan, Forced Breaks, and Grounding

Finally, there are certain behaviors that need more than shaping. Some children develop habits in which they reject the expectations, values, and morals of their family and/or school. On some level, whether unconsciously or with intent, the child seems to "choose" to resist the therapy/ education process and follows her egocentric instincts. She may avoid therapeutic/coaching conversations because they bring up shame, frustration, or anxiety. The child may act in a bullying or harassing manner toward others, due to insecurity, low self-esteem, or as an offensive approach to self-protection.

Some of these repeated behaviors are unsafe, bullying, or completely disruptive to the home or classroom. Others disregard the structure, schedule, and authority of the adult (which can be infuriating for caregivers). Deal Breakers are not single, intense episodes of acting out or emotional reactiveness, and they are not out of control Red Phase behaviors. We are talking about standing patterns of behavior that are negativistic, controlling, and rejecting of the social learning and coaching process. Often the child seems to have a need to feel powerful and tries to dominate others through insulting behavior or by saying "No" to all requests. Examples of these out-of-bounds behaviors include:

- Walking away from the group to do a preferred activity, without permission

- Consistently looking straight at the adult and willfully refusing to cooperate with instructions

- Debating, badgering, and arguing points endlessly, even after the caregiver says, "Enough."

- Maintaining a stance of "I don't care." when you offer social coaching such as perspective taking or problem-solving mistakes

- Ignoring consequences (sneaking smart phone use after losing the privilege, searching the house for the TV remote after you confiscated it)

- Disregarding others' physical and emotional safety, for instance, constantly insulting a sibling or peer and not stopping the behavior when requested by sibling and parents

When these patterns arise, it is as if the child with SECCs has flipped the "I don't care" switch. The child is no longer adhering to the family's values or the school's code of behavior. Her refusal or domination gives her far more power than is healthy or functional. The child is now acting out her own needs on others, which means she is on her *Own Plan*. She has fallen off the *Family Plan* (at home) or the *School Plan* (if it's happening at school). At this point the child needs help getting out of this rut and giving up control. It's likely that, at this point, the child will require every trick in this book and individual therapy, as well.

These are some of the most difficult behaviors to deal with. Caregivers often clamp down and an epic struggle for control breaks out. The child acts out and the caregiver responds with corrections, exasperation, frustration, and increasingly severe consequences. This makes the child tense and angry, which leads to the next round of Deal-Breaking behavior and consequences.

The child who is concrete and struggles to connect her behavior with others' reactions misinterprets the caregiver's corrections: "She's mean." "She doesn't like me." "I hate my mom." "This school sucks." The child is blind to the fact that, on some level, *she is choosing* the negative behavior and her negative outcome. The negative consequence is inevitable, but your child doesn't see her role in it.

This cycle is beyond non-productive; it is destructive. It takes on an adversarial feeling. The child's negativity can take over, and the atmosphere feels tense and awful. Moreover, the child with SECCs is suffering and not learning what you want her to learn. What do you want the child to learn?

- To observe and accept her role in interactions

- To recognize that the world responds to every action she performs

- To read social cues and emotions of others and adjust her behavior accordingly

- To take responsibility for mistakes, to correct, and make amends

- To decrease the instinctive, me-first approach to the world and to open up to social expectations around her

- To participate in therapy or social coaching and problem-solving processes

- To understand it is okay to give up some control and you'll be fine

- To stop the behaviors that are simply not okay

Caregivers need to engage in a peaceful coup to take back authority, control, and leadership. The caregiver is reminded that you are the executive of the "family business" and that the child is the "worker bee" whose job is to learn, play, socialize, and contribute to the larger group.

The child's self-importance and *I can do whatever I want* attitude must be punctured. Children mistakenly believe that they can act as horribly as they want yet are still entitled to all their usual fun and privileges. Adults sometimes get co-opted into this false belief and forget that the child only has the privileges you grant. There is no line in the Bill of Rights that says, "Your lovely child has the inalienable right to ice cream, later bedtimes, and the pursuit of video games." Your child is only entitled to life's necessities, physical and emotional safety, food, water, shelter, and the like. This is your leverage.

To intervene when things get dicey like this, we developed a simple, dramatic, and concrete way to reflect to a child what is happening. Her Iceberg Behavior is *begging* for more swaddling and structure but she won't accept it voluntarily. To turn the tables, we create a dramatic if-then action-reaction consequence. We place the responsibility for the outcome squarely at the feet of the child. It is crucial that the child realizes her self-determination. The response I am about to share communicates to the child her right and responsibility to choose her path. "What's your Road to Happiness?"

Let's look at an example from an interaction with a child at my therapeutic day camp. The camper's name has been changed for confidentiality.

First, establish the concept of the Camper Plan. "Katie, I just figured something out and I want to share it with you. Your counselors and I noticed that you have been deciding not to listen to them very much these days. You have been saying mean things to your group mates. And you've been arguing and walking away when your counselors try to talk to you about it.

[Katie grumbles and averts her eyes, but you keep going.]

It's like you are on the Katie Plan and doing whatever you want. You can choose to stay on the Katie Plan, but you should know what happens when you are on it. It just seems as though on the Katie Plan you are stressed and angry a lot, and you aren't having a very good time. Would you choose to have a bad time?

[Katie's response, "No."]

Then, contrast it with the Family/School/Camp Plan. "We have a problem here. The Katie Plan is way different than the Camp Pegasus Plan. On the Camp Pegasus Plan, *campers enjoy the fun activity schedule and play with friends.* The Camp Pegasus Plan has rules about using kind words and voices. This must be a safe place for all campers. On the Camp Pegasus Plan, you get all that fun when you follow the schedule and the rules, listen to the counselors, and do problem solving to figure out better ways to handle things. When campers are on the Camp Pegasus Plan, camp can be really fun."

Define Deal-Breakers, cause-and-effect and the child's potential consequence. "But you simply can't be mean to other campers or walk away from counselors' directions. Those behaviors are Deal Breakers and are *not okay*. So, starting now, I want to tell you about an important choice you must make. **If** you *choose* to be mean to your bunk mates; **if** you *choose* to ignore your counselors who are only trying to help, **then** you are *choosing* the Katie Plan. **If** you *choose* the Katie Plan, **then** you are *choosing* to be shut down for camp activities and privileges. **If** you decide on the Katie Plan, **then** you decide to ground yourself. *You decide.* In the Katie Plan, you will wind up sitting under a tree or in the office being bored. **If** you *choose* to be on the Camp Pegasus Plan, that means that you *try* to use kind words and a kind voice. You *try* to accept counselors' help and you *try* to follow the rules. **If** you are on the Camp Pegasus Plan, **then** you get to participate in all the activities and earn chips toward your prizes."

Emphasize the child's responsibility and self-determination moving forward. "You are welcome to stay on the Katie Plan for as long as you want. I can't force you to do anything and it's *your choice*. If you find that you are shut down and bored, it is because *you chose* the Katie Plan. Just know that the Katie Plan is boring, and the Camp Pegasus Plan is fun. Good luck. I'm sure you will make exactly the right *choice* for you."

Notice the repetition in the speech emphasizing the contrast between the two plans. Notice the repetition of the words *choice* and *decide*. This approach places all of the responsibility for the child's actions on the child. For the child clutching at control, it is rather disarming. If your child tries to blame you, don't let her make it personal. Stick to your guns. "That's the rule. Look, it's written right here. It's all up to *you*. *You chose* to _____."

Your follow through and consistency is vital to the success of any intervention. Your child should not rejoin the activity or receive full privileges if she reverts to the Deal Breaker behavior. "Oops, you are back on the Katie Plan. You have chosen to ground yourself. You can get ungrounded when you make a plan with me for how you will move forward on the Family Plan." While your child is grounded, check in every so often. "What are you thinking? Which plan will you try? Let me know if you decide to change your mind."

You will need emotional endurance and courage to outlast your child's stubbornness. I've heard of a child grounding herself for three months before realizing she couldn't break down her caregiver. She may grow angrier and threatening initially. She may even visit the Red Phase. Your calm and empathic message is, "You're entitled to be frustrated or angry. Raging won't get you ungrounded. Deciding to cooperate with _____ will get all your privileges back. You decide when you're ready to get back on the Family/School Plan."

Your child must stay grounded until she addresses you personally and relents. "Fine, I'll do the Camp Pegasus Plan." At that point, your child will be somewhat workable. Try to problem solve the feeling or frustration that is under the huge iceberg you have been dealing with.

Lastly, remember our positive cycles. Always be ready to support and reinforce it if your child changes her mind. Get back to TPR + chips and reinforce all the good your child can produce on the Family Plan. Give her credit and congratulate her for taking responsibility and making a powerful decision for herself and the family/group. If you use chips, heap a ton of them on your child, because giving up control is magnificent and difficult. You should provide significant external reinforcement, so your child feels positive about making that difficult choice.

Now you have an answer for every level of your child's social-behavioral challenges.

- You have a plan for routine social miscues with Jeopardy Coaching.

- You can create a holding environment to provide emotional security and containment via Do-Rule and No-Rule lists (including Positive Replacement Behaviors).

- You are now capable of creating a positive-negative behavior reinforcement system.

    o Create positive reinforcement for Increase-Behaviors with TPR plus the Sloppy, Relationship-Based, Carnival-Style Reward System

    o Create negative reinforcement to fade undesired, Decrease-Behaviors with Predictable Logical Consequences

- You can respond in a non-reactive manner to Deal Breaker behavior using the Family/School Plan versus the Child's Plan.

CHAPTER 6

PUTTING IT ALL TOGETHER

The holistic social-coping training method in this book weaves together several intervention strategies for children with SECCs. They have been trialed in homes, schools, therapy offices, and at a therapeutic social skills day camp. Parents and professionals professed gratitude that this approach enhanced relationships with their children, created a positive environment, and facilitated improvement in social and emotional coping skills. Additionally, as of this writing, two psychology doctoral dissertations have studied outcome efficacy of the Camp Pegasus program. The studies demonstrated that Camp Pegasus, which features the strategies from this book, results in clinically significant improvement in social skills and executive functioning skills.

The program's foundation is a loving, person-centered philosophy. It begins with faith that each child is doing his best to navigate life as he is enabled by his social-coping skills. Adult users of the Art of Friendship social training approach celebrate each success. Any successful behavior is made possible by the child's current set of acquired social-coping skills. An ineffective or inappropriate social behavior reveals gaps in underlying cognitive social and coping skills. Caregivers use the Iceberg Theory to infer what underlying social-coping skill needs to be developed. What unwritten social rule or awareness does he need to learn? What social-coping skill does he need to engage socially and to self-regulate?

Caregivers should avoid the "control-contain-punish" philosophy of behavior. It doesn't promote acquisition of skills or the practice of positive replacement behaviors. Life with your child with SECCs should instead be viewed as a teaching and learning process. The caregiver's role is that of a lifelong social coach.

The Art of Friendship program ignites with direct instruction of social awareness, social skills, and emotional coping skills. There wasn't room in this book to share the wide-ranging Art of Friendship Social-Coping Skills Curriculum®. I will share them in a series of subsequent publications under the "Art of Friendship" series banner.

This volume introduced the ultra-positive social-coping skills training approach, featuring:

- Positive cycle creation to reinforce the practice and acquisition of new social-coping skills

  o Writing, publishing and posting (W.P.P.) Increase-Behavior Do-Rules lists

  o Attending to the positive

  o Targeted ignoring

  o Targeted Positive Reflection (TPR)

  o The sloppy, carnival-style, relationship-based behavior reinforcement system

- Compassionate social coaching techniques

  o Jeopardy Coaching

  o Success-oriented instructions

  o Accepting and celebrating baby-steps

  o Creating a Culture of Readiness

- Strategies to provide limits/consequences to decrease or extinguish undesirable behavior

  o W.P.P.'ing "Decrease-Behavior" rule lists

  o Expected/logical consequences

  o If-then cause and effect consequences

- The forced-choice Kid Program versus Family/School Program strategy to manage unsafe or oppositional Deal-Breaker behaviors

Some families say that this is a whole new orientation to caring for their child with SECCs. Other parents tell me that they instinctively tried some of these ideas, but never in the intentional, comprehensive way I lay out. No pressure is intended for you to use every strategy in this book. These are merely a set of helpful ideas, humbly shared. Feel free to cherry pick the ones that most fit your child's needs and development.

Sometimes training and behavior-modification can feel sterile and impersonal. Not the Art of Friendship. It has heart and Therapeutic Love at its core. Remember, delivering Love means to identify *exactly* what a child needs and deliver it with acts of caring. This social-coping skills training program must be individualized to the unique needs of your child. Some children benefit from TPR while others may need chips to power-up the social-coping learning and process. Some children require more structure and limits in the form of written Decrease-Behaviors or logical expected consequences. Some need the "Deal Beaker" intervention. Caring for the child with SECCs can be fraught with worry and stress. It is hard.

I want to share a final drop of wisdom gleaned from over twenty years of treating children with SECCs. Whatever your child's present social-coping ability, *it's temporary.* Your child is always changing. His brain grows more mature and sophisticated every day through his mid- to late twenties. Children move through a predictable developmental sequence of cognitive abilities. I nicknamed the stages of development "Epochs of Mind." Each Epoch pulls the child ever higher to new abilities, perspectives, and urges. Most caregivers I know fret that the challenges by which they are surrounded will always be this way. "How will my child ever _____?" (insert "go to college," "have meaningful relationships," get a job," etc.) You are anxious because you passionately wish that your child will grow up to be okay.

Let me elaborate on the Epochs of Mind. Children begin their social lives using the Preschool Brain in which the child is filled with fantasy, irrationality, and mercurial emotions, and impulses. Then comes the elementary-age Epoch that is more collaborative, occasionally rational, and task oriented. The middle-school brain Epoch triggers an "opening up," which allows an inconsistent acceptance that there are other perspectives and opportunities out there (while revisiting some of the emotional volatility of the first Epoch).

Often, the adolescent Epoch of Mind is a turning point for the child with SECCs. For many of my clients, brain development neutralizes emotional upheavals and triggers the adolescent drive for independence. The child strives to push away from caregivers and realizes that his life is his own. I have seen a child who, in previous Epochs melted down, avoided social settings and had conflicts with others suddenly develop an unexpected personal goal. It was as if his brain suddenly developed an awareness of self and *the future*—and that he could participate in crafting it. This is called self-determination. When children reach the Adolescent Epoch of Mind, they often seem to become more invested in treatment and more collaborative in goal setting and baby-stepping.

These Epochs of Mind are not set to chronological age. It would be unethical for me to falsely promise that your child will hit all these stages. I certainly can't guarantee that your child will hit each Epoch on cue when he transitions to each level of education. However, the developmental flow I repeatedly witness gives me hope for each child.

When I first began working with this population, I imagined a "glass ceiling." I sometimes had limiting beliefs such as, "This child will only be able to achieve _____" based on my early observations of their abilities and challenges. Twenty years of experience and wisdom shattered my mental glass ceiling. I gained a new perspective from long-term treatment with children from single digits through high school graduation. A few have even returned to work with me as young adults, enabling me to reflect on their developmental arcs.

One young client spent fourth grade in the fetal position under his classroom desk, only ate Hot Pockets, and never electively left the house. Then, his brain reached the Adolescent Epoch around age 16. He asked to graduate from high school early and enroll in college. Today he works behind the scenes as a coder for the website of a major news organization. He lives in a large city in an apartment and has friends and a girlfriend. His loving parents and I had no way to predict this is where his life would lead.

Another client of mine battled with her parents at every turn, melted down through middle school, refused to do routine hygiene (especially hair care due to sensory discomfort and motor coordination issues). This continued deep into high school. Today she works as a medical aide and has a long-term boyfriend and an apartment. Her hair looks great.

Life isn't perfect or easy for these two young adult clients, and their SECCs still provide challenges. On the positive side, they have their own independent lives. They are happy and proud to be out there living them. They are just like you and me, doing their best to make it each day. They are living proof that there is no glass ceiling.

How did these children become productive members of society? It was a combination of everything they experienced growing up. Ongoing brain growth pulled them forward to each Epoch of Mind. Each year their new teachers *stayed engaged* with their needs and used the Art of Friendship strategies I taught them. Their parents and caregivers *stayed engaged* with the process, even when they felt overwhelmed or hopeless. I *stayed engaged* with them and guided everyone to celebrate each success and work on each new skill gap that presented itself.

There were downs and there were ups. Each client experienced one or more bouts of deep depression and/or panic attacks, respectively. One was traumatized by two different bullies at different epochs. My clients' growth was usually fitful: two steps forward, three steps back, seven steps forward, two steps back, and so on. It is non-linear growth, *but it is growth.*

Here is my take-away. *There is hope.* Yes, there is no way to predict the future, but there is hope. The way your child functions today will not guarantee a certain outcome tomorrow. There is no way to predict the rate of his brain growth. There is no way to anticipate when, or if, he will seize the reins of his own life and forge his own goals. But there is hope.

We should not pre-decide how far a child can grow based on our own pessimism or anxiety. All we can do is *stay engaged*. We must bring the presence of our full being to the task, which means mind, body, and heart. Celebrate each success and growth step. When there are struggles and failures, hang in there and model resilience and hope. Tell your child about your own failures and struggles and demonstrate that they don't define you. Accept your child for who he is today and keep a hopeful eye on tomorrow. Don't get too far ahead of yourself with expectations or worries. Keep your mind focused on the present and proactively plan in one-year blocks. What will he need next?

CONCLUSION

It is my passionate dream to decrease people's struggle and contribute to a better world. It's what I was put on this earth to do. I learned so much about life, socialization, and relationships from the clients, parents, and professionals with whom I have had the honor of working. Writing this book has been a long, long labor of love. It is my gift to you. I pray that you find this to be a powerful force of growth for your child, family, or group.

Once you incorporate the Art of Friendship social training skills into your repertoire, please think of another person in your orbit who may benefit from it and pass this book on. We can make a better world together.

You got this. Onward and upward.

ACKNOWLEDGEMENTS

I offer my deep gratitude to the creative team that assisted with the publication of this, my first book. Editor extraordinaire, Louis Greenstein, guided me through my inaugural book editing process and polished my ideas into efficient and clear prose. Brenda Lange, my outstanding proofreader applied her laser-focus on granular details of punctuation and consistency, ensuring a high-quality professional product. My mother, Marilyn Fogel, who has been proofreading my writing since I could write, took the final turn and made sure the text was perfect and that I didn't overuse exclamation marks (!). Jamie Amen, my longtime graphic designer created the attractive book cover as well as the Think-Feel-Do Problem Solving Worksheet and the Emotional GPS images included herein. She always makes my business and programs look amazing and outdid herself on this project.

This volume reverberates with the inspiration and wisdom of two mentors who launched my adult and professional life. Ron Hays and Dr. Nancy Gerber, my "art therapy parents", charged me to pursue insight. They preached moving beyond "techniques", in lieu of the therapeutic relationship, which is the true engine of healing and growth. Ron challenged my default attitude of *ignorance is bliss* and provided the contrary epiphany that insight and awareness is bliss. When we're aware of our own reactions and patterns, we have true freedom and we're freed from the bondage of habit. Best of all, we become empowered to choose successful *new* behaviors that lead to healing and self-actualization. Nancy was my Yoda. She supercharged my work with children and adolescents by introducing me to therapeutic storytelling, enhancing my mastery of empathic visual communication, and guiding my formation of deep therapeutic relationships with clients. This book is the flowering of seeds planted by these inspirational educators years ago.

I am thankful to be on this helping journey with my professional family, the brilliant art therapists who work(ed) at the Child and Family Art Therapy Center and the inspiring staff at Camp Pegasus. Your love of childhood reinforces mine, and your challenging questions ensure that I continuously learn and grow. Your like-minded dedication to making the world a better place, your laughter, and your teamwork breathes warm winds of hope into my sails.

Lisa, Emily, and Sam, you are my breath, my food, my drink, and my shelter. As an adolescent I had no professional goals and only wanted to be a great husband and father. You are my dreams come true. Lisa, you are my love, my best friend and partner-in-everything, and shower me with just the right doses of encouragement and grounding. Nothing I do outside the home is possible without your support. Emmy and Sammy, you are the greatest works of art I ever had a hand in creating (you did most of the work, you know!). I am your biggest fan and am so proud of the adults you are becoming. My entire family supported my career and enthusiastically encouraged this project. You graciously found patience for yet another camp story or my excited description of a new social lesson. Everything I do, I do as a representative of you and our family. I strive every day to make you proud (except when I embarrass you on purpose). Anything is possible if you dare to dream and follow your dream with baby-step actions!

An immense debt of gratitude goes to all the clients I ever had the honor of treating. You always remind me of my humanity. To be human is to grapple with life and emotions, and there is honor and inspiration in the struggle. I also wrestle with life and have many skills to learn! It turns out my clients reveal to ME my own social skills gaps. By following my own advice to them, I became a more successful person, family member, professional, and entrepreneur!

Finally, I thank all the parents who entrusted me with your precious children. Your questions, critiques, and requests were rocket fuel for my constant program improvement. You challenged me to constantly enhance my communication about your child's inner experiences and needs. Your hunger for real-world support strategies sparked my research and creativity. For over two decades, you drove my evolution from face to face parent meetings, to local seminars, to conference presentations, and the publication of this book. My rewarding experiences with your child and you taught me more than I can ever share in a thousand books.

I wouldn't be the man or the professional I am today without all of you.

With infinite gratitude, Mike

ABOUT THE AUTHOR

Mike Fogel, MA, ATR-BC, LPC, is passionate about children, parenting, and playfulness in therapy. Inspired to create a better world, Mike, a licensed professional counselor and art therapist, innovated award-winning child therapy programs and businesses: The Art of Friendship Social-Coping Program® (2000), the Child and Family Art Therapy Center (2007), Camp Pegasus (2013), and the BetterWorld Affordable Art Therapy Program (2019). In 2006, he received the "Innovative Application of Art Therapy Award" from the Pennsylvania Art Therapy Association.

Mike holistically addresses a child's entire inner world and formative environment in therapy. Creativity, visual communication, play, and humor are Mike's tools to foster the ideal atmosphere for children and adolescents to heal and overcome a wide range of emotional-behavioral challenges. Mike's work is supercharged by heartfelt faith that every person has the innate capacity to heal, grow, and progress toward their vast personal potential, and his parents and clients "get that."

Since 2000, Mike cultivated a specialty in social skills group therapy with neuro-diverse children with High Functioning Autism, ADHD, and learning differences. The unique needs of this population stimulated Mike's creation of The Art of Friendship Social-Coping Program®. Mike continues to facilitate weekly social-coping skills therapy groups, out of which, an original Art of Friendship social-coping skill curriculum organically evolved. As it turns out, most caregivers who learn Mike's techniques and social-coping skills language say that people of *any* age can benefit from these lessons. Mike's year-round social skills group therapy work is enhanced by his therapeutic social skills summer day camp, Camp Pegasus. Mike's warm, loving style engages even the most reluctant client or camper, and his training style presents complex concepts in clear and memorable ways.

Mike was a long-time adjunct professor and clinical supervisor in Drexel University's Hahnemann graduate art therapy program, and he remains involved in clinical education. You can find Mike teaching at conferences and workshops around the country, where he is a popular presenter on creative and visual ways to help children and families overcome challenges and thrive. He served in volunteer positions on the board of directors of the Asperger & Autism Alliance of Greater Philadelphia and the Pennsylvania Art Therapy Association. Presently, Mike is thrilled to fulfill his dream of sharing his game-changing and creative lessons worldwide through publication and presentation.

Mike lives near Philadelphia, Pennsylvania, with his wife, two children, and Penny the Shih-Tsu. He loves comic books, progressive rock music, all things comedic, St. Joseph's University basketball (The Hawk Will Never Die), and his Philadelphia Eagles.

This powerful training expands on the techniques laid out in *The Social Emotional Guidebook*

Unpacking the Social-Emotional Guidebook: Motivating children with social challenges to practice social & emotional coping skills

Presentation options:

~Two-hour keynote
~Half day
~Whole day
~Two day

Mike offers in-service programs and presentations on a variety of subjects related to child development, mental health, bullying, social development, and parenting issues. If you are interested in having him present for your group or event, please contact him at Guidebook@ ChildAndFamilyArtTherapyCenter.com

Speaking engagements:
Mike Fogel, MA, ATR-BC, LPC, is an innovative therapist, author and speaker whose passionate goal is to make the world a better place, one child and family at a time. He is known as a charismatic and engaging speaker, whose presentations to parents and professionals are eagerly anticipated and well-attended. He presents at national and local conferences and for professional and lay organizations, teaching various caregiver skill areas, helping kids with anxiety, frustration/anger, etc. Mike's knowledge, positivity and caring shine, as he makes complex social and psychological concepts crystal clear and memorable—always with plenty of humor. His practical strategies can be implemented immediately; audience members have reported great success when they put his lessons into practice in their home or office.

Mike's most popular presentations for parents, educators, and professionals:

Support techniques for parents, educators, and caregivers as stand-alone presentations or combined with one from the next section.

A. *The Art of Friendship: Secret Ingredients of Social Skills Training for Parents, Professionals & Educators* (1-4 hours) (may be with combined with B, 1, 2, 4, 5)

B. *Love with Limits: Structure & Behavior Modification Techniques to Increase Positive Coping & Decrease Challenging Behaviors* (1-4 hours) (may be combined with A, 1, 2, 3, 4)

Social and emotional coping skill modules provide parents and professionals child/adolescent-friendly language and a visual framework to teach social and coping skills. All of these programs can be combined to create a unique presentation for your group.

1. *Meltdowns and Shut-downs! Helping Children Develop Frustration Tolerance & Anger Management Skills* (1-3 hours)

2. *The Road to Happiness: Developing Assertiveness and Problem-Solving Skills in Children* (1-3 hours)

3. *Counter-Intuitive Caregiving: Helping Children Cope with Anxiety, Worry & Stress (1-3 hours)*

4. *"The Team for Fun"- Introduction to Social Skills Training* (key concepts and skills) (1-3 hours)

5. *The Personal Power Project: Helping Children Stand Up to Bullies, Teasers, and Impossible Kids* (1-2 hours)

Don't miss this "meta" presentation for professionals and educators:

Art Therapy in Reverse: Visual Communication with Children with Processing Differences (ASD, ADHD, and Learning Differences) (2-4 hours)

This program focuses on children with processing differences. Specifically, Mike shares how they often become cognitively/emotionally overloaded when caregivers rely on a great deal of verbal communication when teaching, disciplining, providing verbal therapy, coaching, etc. Out of Mike's clinical experience as an art therapist working with children with neuro-diverse processing styles, he developed a visual language with his clients to help them understand difficult and abstract social-emotional concepts. Mike shares a step-by step and repeatable system of visual communication for anyone to use with their students and clients.

<u>Subscribe to Mike Fogel's Art of Friendship YouTube channel</u>
for a trove of parent support videos

Discover visually based social-coping techniques and coaching strategies for people of all ages.

- Coping with anxiety

- Defeating negative and depressive thinking

- Managing frustration, anger, and meltdowns

- Strategies for reinforcing social-coping skill development

- Behavior management plans to increase positive coping & cooperation while decreasing unhelpful or destructive behavior

- And much, much more

Printed in the United States
By Bookmasters